Dayton Ghosts

Karen Laven

with Doug Laven

Schiffer Publishing Ltd

4880 Lower Valley Road   Atglen, Pennsylvania   19310

Schiffer Books are available at special discounts for bulk purchases for sales promotions or premiums. Special editions, including personalized covers, corporate imprints, and excerpts can be created in large quantities for special needs. For more information contact the publisher:

Published by Schiffer Publishing Ltd.
4880 Lower Valley Road
Atglen, PA 19310
Phone: (610) 593-1777; Fax: (610) 593-2002
E-mail: Info@schifferbooks.com

For the largest selection of fine reference books on this and related subjects, please visit our web site at **www.schifferbooks.com**
We are always looking for people to write books on new and related subjects. If you have an idea for a book please contact us at the above address.

This book may be purchased from the publisher.
Include $5.00 for shipping.
Please try your bookstore first.

You may write for a free catalog.

In Europe, Schiffer books are distributed by
Bushwood Books
6 Marksbury Ave.
Kew Gardens
Surrey TW9 4JF England
Phone: 44 (0) 20 8392-8585; Fax: 44 (0) 20 8392-9876
E-mail: info@bushwoodbooks.co.uk
Website: www.bushwoodbooks.co.uk
Free postage in the U.K., Europe; air mail at cost.

Ghost image (page 129) adapted from Celebration of Love Oracle Card by Eva-Sakmar Sullivan,
www.stardolphin.com.

Designed by RoS
Type set in Papyrus/ Zurich BT

ISBN: 978-0-7643-3196-1

Printed in The United States of America

Dedication

For my sister, Krissy.
12/56 - 4/08
I love you and miss you.

Acknowledgments

Thank you...

Thank you to my husband, Doug, for tooling us from Northern Kentucky to Dayton and back on numerous occasions (and we only got lost three or seven times!). Thank you, also, for being so hands on with this book; taking photos, interviewing people, and helping track down leads. Pretty soon you'll be authoring your own titles; until then, I'm very grateful that we make such a great authoring team. Thanks to Robin Albright and the Dayton Ghost Hunters Society. Your help and expertise was much appreciated. Thank you also to Sean McHugh for your nifty illustrations for this book; they are awesome! Thanks, too, goes to my kids for putting up with me (again) while I come close to deadline. Thanks, J.T. Ryder for showing us your town and providing your own paranormal experiences. Thanks to my fellow Schiffer author (and buddy) Sherry Strub. You know how much your support means to me. And to my editor Dinah Roseberry; you are a writer's dream! Of course, I thank all of you who shared your true accounts for this book with such candor and grace. I couldn't have done it without you. And, finally, thanks to you, the reader. I appreciate each and every one of you.

Contents

Author's Note

Some of the names in this book have been changed at the interviewee's request. These include the individuals featured in Chapters 2, 7, 12, 14, 30, and 34. The titles of certain structures in Dayton have been changed in chapters 17 and 22 in order to protect the privacy of those persons currently residing there.

Introduction

Dayton's Paranormal Side

Dayton, Ohio (aka, The Gem City and the Birthplace of Aviation), is a soaring example of innovation and dedication to inventiveness. This proud (and wonderfully haunted) town, situated on the Great Miami River, is located about an hour north of Cincinnati in the southwestern section of the state at the "Crossroads of America," where the I-75 north/south meets the I-70 east/west.

The Dayton area is large and growing; encompassing four counties (Montgomery, Miami, Clark, and Green) and holding close to a million residents. Soon, Dayton and Cincinnati will be connected as Cincinnati's growth continues to tentacle further north into the Miami Valley region. When this is complete, it will rank as one of the top twenty largest metropolitan areas in the country. Dayton's surrounding metropolitan locale currently includes communities like Kettering, Miamisburg, Medway, Urbana, Germantown, Centerville, Xenia, Yellow Springs, Springboro, and Beavercreek.

This metropolis located in southwestern Ohio was founded by a small group of settlers in 1796 and named after Jonathon Dayton, a Captain in the American Revolutionary War (who also signed the U.S. Constitution).

The area was a prime spot for the Native Americans to roam and there are several large Indian mounds in the vicinity. Many people I interviewed for the book recounted their proximity to such mounds and their suspicions that this held a clue to the hauntings they were experiencing. Perhaps this is one of the reasons that no matter whether you go north, east, west, or south in the Dayton area, you are bound to uncover a haunted locale.

As is the case with many midsized cities, Daytonites have undergone their share of hardships and struggles over the last century. One major example is the Great Dayton Flood, which occurred in 1913. It was late wintertime when the Great Miami River, unable to hold approximately ten inches of rain in a three-day drench, released its contents upon the land. The surrounding ground was still frozen, which eliminated its abilities to absorb the overflow. Several hundred people perished in this catastrophe, and to make things worse, gas lines broke and part of downtown Dayton burned as a result.

An apparition (a man and his mules) believed to be a casualty of this flood is featured in this book. It was a horrific time, but also aptly showcases the area's ingrained innovation. For it was directly in the wake of the flood that residents pulled up their collective bootstraps and raised $2 million to begin building a dam system and adeptly garnered further funds to finish the job.

The flood's aftermath also ultimately led to the Probable Maximum Flood standard—a standard that is still utilized by civil engineers a century later to aid in their design of flood control systems. The concept and creation of the first hydro lab occurred back then, and hydro labs are still used by the Army Corps of Engineers to test their methods to this day. Dayton residents' actions, strengths, and resolve in the aftermath of this disaster changed how all floods are managed forever.

Willingness to face down the seemingly impossible and rise above adversity is witnessed time and time again in Dayton history. The Wright Brothers exemplify this beautifully. Of course Dayton is referred to as the birthplace of aviation because it is where those infamous high-flying brothers, Wilbur and Orville Wright, hail from. The dreams, aspirations, and talents of these two fellows figuratively and literally took flight. The self-taught pair initially owned and operated a bicycle shop in town and, over the years, concocted and then somehow amazingly erected the first ever power-driven, sustained-flight aircraft. They spent countless hours creating and tweaking their achievement in 1904 to 1905, and then launched it in Kitty Hawk, North Carolina.

Inventing prowess seems to be simmering in the Great Miami River in Dayton as many in the area and surrounding parts tend to exhibit incredible inventive proclivity. Truth is, more patents are issued there, per capita, than any other American city. Charles Kettering, who was also from Dayton, is a fine example of productivity and ingenuity. He was the holder of more than 300 patents and is part of inventing the electric starter motor for automobiles. He is also connected with inventing leaded gasoline and Freon™. We visit a haunted house in Kettering later in this book.

James J. Ritty, also from Dayton, invented the first cash register. The National Cash Register Company was founded in Dayton and remains one of the leading business equipment manufacturers in the world.

Although it is a midsize town, Dayton played a part during World War II via the Dayton Project. The local chemical company devised a means to industrially produce the chemical polonium, which was utilized in the triggers of atomic bombs. Also during this time, the National Cash Register Company's employees, among other things, erected airplane engines and secretly concocted code-breaking machines, including the model that was pivotal in cracking the Enigma machine.

Most recently, Dayton was the site for the Dayton Agreement: the peace accord negotiated at Wright Patterson Air Force Base (per the conflict in Bosnia and former Yugoslavia).

Much of the most-prized history of the area involves flight (aptly so) and the Wright Patterson Air Force Museum (soaringly haunted— hold onto your propellers!) has a fine display of the Wright brothers' achievements as does the Dayton Aviation Heritage Park (Wright Brothers Aviation Center) and the Wright Cycle Company Building. The Wright Brothers are entombed at the delightfully haunted Woodland Cemetery. Given its size, it seems that Dayton has more than its share of well-known Daytonites.

The brilliant humorist, columnist, and author Erma Bombeck (*If Life is a Bowl of Cherries, What Am I Doing in the Pits?*, McGraw-Hill, 1978) was born and bred in Dayton and is buried at Woodland, as well. African American poet, novelist, and playwright Paul Lawrence Dunbar hailed from the Dayton area and, yes, his final resting place is at Woodland; but his influence lives on. Dunbar, through his writings, is credited with feeding the transference of the identity and social consciousness of the African American community throughout America.

Other well-known people from the Dayton area include Major League Baseball players Mike Schmidt and Roger Clemens, actor Gordon Jump and Gary Sandy (two *WKRP in Cincinnati* alumni), actress Allison Janney, actors Chad Lowe and Martin Sheen. And did you know that Phil Donahue started his talk show initially as a local offering in good old Dayton?

Dayton certainly can exude a smaller town feel but it also has plenty of cultural activities to witness and take part in. Organizations such as the Dayton Ballet and the Dayton Art Institute are fine examples of this. The area also offers the Benjamin and Marina Schuster and the Dayton Cultural Center. There are sports, of course, as well. Ready to root for the home team? Watch them sink hoops during the University of Dayton Flyer's basketball games and there is also the Dayton Dragons, a minor league baseball team swinging hard to keep the fans cheering at Fifth Third Field. There are other options too, including the Gem City Rollergirls (a women's roller derby league).

Dayton has a variety of attractions and activities outdoors including fly fishing, cycling, canoeing, kayaking, backpacking, hiking, and more.

To be honest, the area is bouncing back from some difficult economic times; many buildings have been abandoned, but the city is working to reinvent itself yet again. Residents seem fiercely loyal to their town, even while acknowledging there are difficulties still to overcome.

J.T. Ryder, a writer and Daytonite who is constantly pushing for revival of his town, has stumbled upon a multitude of potentially haunted locales in the area while he was driving a cab and working for a security company, just to name a few of his gigs. In this book, we talk with Ryder about his time within the local abandoned mansion and also as a teenager at an old Shaker site in town.

The community has made it a point to hang onto and refurbish some of their historical buildings such as The Old Courthouse (which still holds the old gallows and is divinely haunted, as it should be) and this energizes the present and future while preserving the past.

There are loads of haunted sites in the Dayton area and there always seem to be more hovering in the shadows.

To start things off, Chapter One of *Dayton Ghosts* will highlight our interview with Robin Albright, president of the Dayton Ghost Hunters Society (DGHS). Albright will get everyone up to speed on just what constitutes a ghost, spirit, and the like, and will also delve into the specifics of how DGHS goes about hunting down (up?) their paranormal cohorts. We get the scoop on the latest gadgets and gizmos as well as what to look for when you are searching for that elusive apparition. So flip the page and let's see what the great metropolis of Dayton has to offer; paranormally speaking, that is.

Chapter 1

The Nuts and Bolts of Ghosts (and Ghost Hunting)

An Interview with Robin Albright
President of the Dayton Ghost Hunters Society (DGHS)

Daytonian Robin Albright puts an extra spin on what being busy entails. Albright juggles an amazing plethora of activities. She owns several business ventures, including a new age shop called Whispering Moon Designs, and she is also a Licensed Massage Therapist and a Reiki Master and Teacher. Fitting snugly into the mix are her duties as the President of the Dayton Ghost Hunters Society (DGHS). Participation in DGHS is technically a labor of love for Albright, yet her passion and time input for the group and what they accomplish and stand for delves far deeper than that.

The DGHS guide states that they are a "non-profit network of ghost hunters and researchers who conduct investigations of the paranormal in a scientific manner. One of our main goals is to seek out allegedly haunted locations and to assist those who are experiencing problems with the paranormal."

The group is professional, caring, and darn thorough, and are affiliated with the American Ghost Society. They take their responsibilities seriously. "Group members search for authentic evidence of the paranormal using various scientific equipment, and try to determine if the location is haunted," notes the guide. "We are seeking genuine evidence and are careful about the presentation of this evidence, insuring that it is legitimate, researched and analyzed before it is presented to the public."

As Albright echoed several times during the interview process, "The credibility of the group is maintained above all else. We do not claim to be experts. No matter what anyone claims, no experts exist when it comes to the supernatural. We work to present an image of competent researchers who are collecting the most authentic evidence possible."

Becoming an active member of DGHS takes dedication. "Active members must complete the Level I and II Investigator Training Program prior to participating in private/residential investigations," notes the DGHS Guide. "Three tiers of certification are offered consisting of several training levels within each certification."

DGHS President Albright took some time to sit down and answer a hodgepodge of questions pertaining to the paranormal—everything from the basics of her group's equipment needs and operational techniques to delving into the meat and potatoes of what types of paranormal entities are out there. She's exuberant, intelligent, and interesting, so let's get started!

Q: How long has your group been in existence?

The Dayton Ghost Hunter's Society was founded in September 2002 by Howard Collins.

Q: How long have you, personally, been ghost hunting?

I have been a member of this group since it began. I have been interested in the paranormal since I was a child. This group was the first formal investigative group I was with.

Q: How many members are in your group?

Twenty-eight (28) Active Members (Trained Investigators) and numerous Associate Members.

Q: What types of entities do you believe are out there?

If you start looking, you will find differing opinions on the definitions of what constitutes a "ghost," "apparition," or "spirit." Some people use these terms interchangeably. Here is how I would describe them:

Ghost

The energy of a person, animal, or object, which has left a "psychic imprint" on our plane of existence. This often can be compared to a movie clip being played over and over. A ghost typically does not interact with the person observing the phenomena, but appears to just go on about its business oblivious of the fact that anyone is watching.

Events associated with ghosts are often referred to as "residual hauntings," i.e., leftover energy. This energy can manifest itself in different ways such as:

Visually: Often occurs when the "ghost" was involved in repetitive activity during life. An example would be someone in life who worked for many years in the same job and after death was still showing up for work…only now in the form of energy! Another form of visual apparition is often associated with a location where great emotional trauma occurred, such as on battlefields.

Sounds: A common auditory manifestation is that of footsteps being heard and no one is there. This was the case at one investigation we did where the client heard footsteps coming down the stairs as he sat in the living room and then, as if the apparition walked across the room and out the door, the front door flew open. Other commonly heard ghostly noises are rappings and voices, but we also hear of things such as the *clip-clop* of horses hooves coming down the street in an area where living horses no longer pull carriages. Battlefields are again common areas for auditory phenomena to occur.

Odors: They say that nothing evokes a memory more strongly than a particular odor. Maybe that is why the imprints of some ghosts appear in the form of olfactory energy. An elderly woman who wore lavender perfume everyday may leave behind psychic energy in the form of lavender scent wafting through a room she frequented. These manifestations are, once again, often associated with repetitive activity in life. Some other examples are pipe tobacco, the smell of bread baking, indicating the person while living did a lot of baking, roses or other floral scents and perfumes.

Did you feel that?: It is quite common to hear someone say that they feel cold spots, or a cold breeze moving through a supposedly haunted location. Although this is one manifestation of paranormal energy, as an investigator, you must be sure to "debunk" this evidence by checking for cold air returns and air conditioning vents, not to mention drafty, poorly sealed old windows.

Spirits

I like to differentiate between the terms "ghost" and "spirit" by whether or not the entity communicates with the living. A ghost would be the energy "imprint" only and would not interact with the living. A spirit is linked to the personality and soul of the individual. For one reason or another, this "personality" has remained in the physical plane and reacts with the living. Some possible reasons for a spirit to linger include staying behind to complete unfinished business, wishing to communicate with the living to give them a message, and the spirit not realizing that it has died. Paranormal events involving entities of this sort are often referred to as "intelligent hauntings."

Poltergeists

The accepted definition of poltergeist has evolved over time. German in origin, the term originally meant "noisy ghost." Thus, for many years, poltergeist activity was thought to be caused exclusively by ghostly activity. Now, you frequently hear that the often-destructive activity (rappings, objects flying across the room, etc.) is caused by an adolescent girl in the home. This is narrowing the field down too far. It can be due to any individual who is under extreme emotional turmoil, stress, etc. Unfortunately, there are many cases of an adolescent, child, or other member of the household actually "faking" the poltergeist activity with all of the finesse of an accomplished magician. This is why a thorough debunking job must be done with all data collected in these cases.

Q: What was the most haunted site you've encountered thus far?

An apartment in the Miamisburg (Ohio) area.

Q: What sorts of evidence did you come away with?

As we've just completed this investigation, we are in the process of analyzing the audio and video data. We had numerous high readings with the K-II meter in the room that the residents had identified as the area where most of the alleged paranormal activity occurs. Residents of the apartment said that most of the activity occurs between 2 – 5 am, with the highest concentration being around 3 am. The investigation started at 9 pm and nothing showed up on any of the meters until approximately 3 am. After 3 am, dowsing rods reacted very strongly in that room and the K-II meter lights appeared to flash on in response to questions being asked. Numerous attempts to debunk the readings failed to turn up anything in the room (lights, electronic equipment, etc.) that was causing the spike. There were also incidences of batteries being drained of power and electronic equipment disruption. Alleged activity as reported by the residents included footsteps heard on the stairs, lights and TV turning on by themselves, and the sighting of a small child on more than one occasion in the same room where the K-II EMF activity was recorded.

Q: Please list the equipment you use at the investigations and describe what their purpose is and how they are utilized.

Cameras: 35M and Digital. You need to understand the limitations (for example, no negative available for analysis, etc.).

Video: Remote camera system with computer. Usually use four remote infrared cameras with built-in microphones, but the system is capable of supporting more cameras if needed.

Main computer and monitor: Set up at the "Tech Station" where the Lead Tech can view input from all four cameras at once. (A typical investigation generates at least twenty hours of video that needs to be reviewed at a later date.)

Regular video cameras: With infrared capability and tripods.

Audio Recorders: Used not only for capturing EVPs (Electronic Voice Phenomena)[EVP is communication via the spirits using tape recorders, radios, video equipment, and alternate electric audio machinery.], but also handy for recording your observations. (Make sure you take plenty of extra batteries along!)

Digital, cassette (w/microphones, adapters, etc.), micro-cassette can be used.

Electro-magnetic Field Detectors (EMF meters): The theory is that paranormal activity will disrupt the electromagnetic field in the area being investigated.

Video Remote System Infrared Camera used by the Dayton Ghost Hunters Society.

Tri-field Meter: Detects changes in Electromagnetic, Radio and Microwave fields.

Natural EM Meter: Very sensitive. We usually place it in a stationary position and use a baby monitor to send the signal back to the Tech Station.

Gauss Master: Very easy to use. Audio signal makes it good for use in dimly-lit locations. Automatically shuts off. [A Gauss Master is used to measure the magnetic fields emitted by everyday electrical appliances and equipment.]

K-II (also called K-2) Meter: Has an array of lights that signal changes in electromagnetic fields and is useful for asking questions and receiving answers based on blinking lights.

Thermometers: Standard. Base unit plus three remote indoor/outdoor thermometers (Base unit kept at Tech Station, three remotes placed in other rooms, but readings can all be taken from base unit.).

Geiger Counter: Detects radiation. The theory is that the presence of paranormal activity in an area might cause a change in radiation levels.

Dowsing Rods: As there is no numeric "scale" attached to dowsing rods, the results are largely subjective and some view them as having limited use. Dowsing rods have been used throughout history to find "hidden" items. Examples include using dowsing rods to detect underground water, mineral deposits, and unmarked graves and to detect paranormal activity.

Misc. Equipment: Flashlights, extra batteries for everything, video/audio tapes, clipboards, pens/pencils, level, power strip and extension cord, radios/walkie-talkies.

Q: What single piece of equipment is most important to you/your investigations in your opinion, and why?

The paper and pencil/pen you use to document your observations, equipment readings, etc., during the investigation. An investigation is only as good as the documentation generated by the investigators. For example: An equipment reading alone tells you very little without knowing when it occurred, where it occurred, who was there, and what else was happening at the same time, along with what steps were taken to "debunk" the data. Some use a tape recorder for this purpose, but with the tendency of batteries to be drained of power and electronic equipment malfunctioning at investigations, the old-fashioned way may be a better option.

Q: What does a typical investigation for you entail?

When a client contacts our group about a potential investigation, they are first put in touch with our Investigative Coordinator who through a phone interview ascertains the feasibility of conducting an investigation at that location.

The Investigative Coordinator assigns a Lead Investigator and Lead Equipment Tech and they conduct an on-site interview with the client.

During the interview, complete details about the paranormal activity are collected and as much of the history of the location as the client can tell us. Baseline EMF readings and photos are taken and a basic site map drawn. A date is set for the first investigation and release forms are signed.

Once a date is set, the Investigative Coordinator assigns Investigators to work on the team. The team typically consists of the Lead Investigator, Lead Equipment Tech, two experienced Investigators and two newer Investigators. Experienced

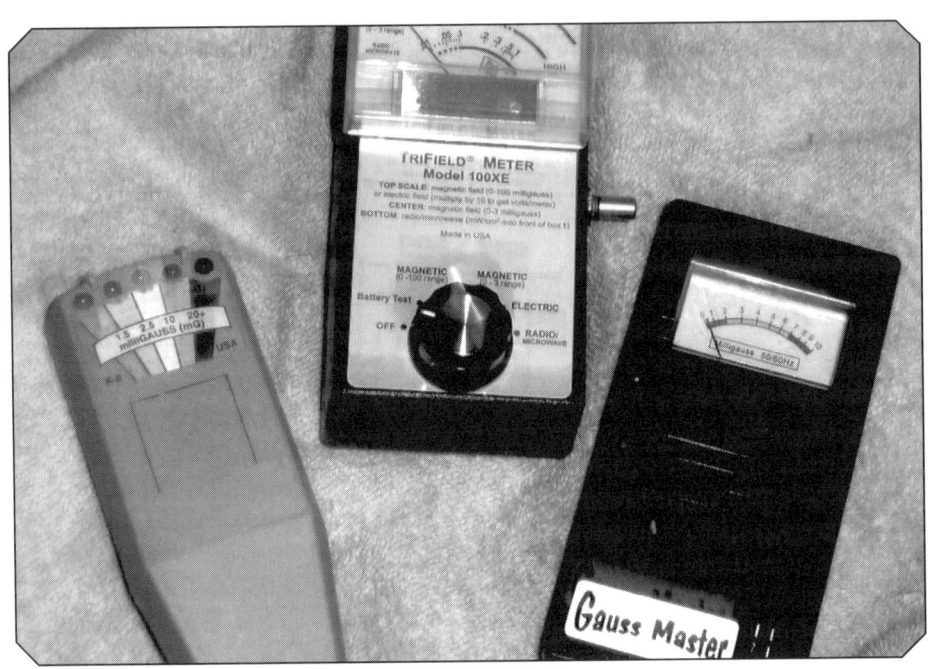

DGHS array of Gauss Meters.

Investigators are paired with those less experienced for training purposes.

Equipment, documentation paperwork, and supplies are assembled and a pre-investigation meeting is held and assignments handed out.

Upon arriving at the site, the remote cameras, thermometers, and other equipment are set up and the team members begin collecting data.

A typical investigation lasts about five hours. After the investigation is over, evidence must be reviewed and "debunked." A decision is made as to whether or not the evidence warrants a second investigation at the site and a final report is developed.

Q: Have you ever been (seriously) afraid while out investigating?

No...only fascinated. The living are far scarier than the dead!

Q: What tips would you give those who want to check some of the sites out themselves?

Always get permission of the property owners before you venture onto private property. Always treat other people's property and businesses with respect. Do not be disruptive to the business if you are attempting to investigate a public location. Do not ever investigate alone...always be sure someone knows where you are.

Keep a clear head...alcohol and drugs have no place at an investigation. Smoking is also not a good idea as it may mask any paranormal "odors" that may have otherwise been detected (Example: Some haunted locations have had incidences where the smell of roses, lavender, sulfur, pipe tobacco, etc. have been detected).

Know your equipment and beware of false equipment readings.

Try to maintain a balance of both an open mind and healthy skepticism. It is best to do some basic research on a location before you investigate. (Again, always take extra batteries!)

Q: What is the most common evidence you come away with?

The most common paranormal happening that we witness during investigations is the "draining" of batteries and disruption of electronic equipment with no apparent cause. In one notable case, we had three separate video cameras shut down at the same time only a short time after the taping began. If all three had been plugged into electrical outlets, an argument could be made that it was caused by an electrical surge or brief disruption of service. However, one camera was operating on a fully-charged battery, one was plugged into a wall outlet, and the third camera was plugged into an outlet, but also had battery backup. The cameras were not all on the same floor in the house, let alone in the same room.

We have also had incidences where brand new batteries in several different types of equipment (flashlight, voice recorder, and radio, for example) were all drained of power within minutes of each other. The ambient temperature and other conditions were not such to have caused the power drain. When things get really exciting is when things like this happen in the same room that the EMF meter spikes, a member of the group has a visual sighting, and the temperature drops. Anytime multiple things happen in the same place, and especially at the same time, the stronger the evidence is. The interesting thing is that it sometimes happens that after the investigation is over and you are back home, the equipment functions perfectly and the batteries are fine.

Q: What is your take on orbs in photographs?

Very skeptical. Most orbs can be debunked as being dust or reflections that the camera picks up. The only orb I would tend to believe might be paranormal is one in which the photo was taken using natural light (no flash). Orbs really show up in video shot in the dark with an IR capable video camera... and dust can behave in a decidedly un-dust-like manner when caught on film. However, just because an orb can be debunked as being caused by dust, it doesn't mean that there was not also a ghost present in the room.

Unfortunately, the "evidence" that most amateur investigators come away with are photographs/video with orbs in them. As most orbs are caused by dust, this is not very compelling evidence. The unreliability of orb "evidence" does not mean that the location is not haunted, just that the orb in the photo is most likely not caused by spiritual energy. We have had several incidences where an investigator saw an orb move through the room with his/her own eyes instead of via the camera lens. That is much more exciting!

Q: Do you more often get contacted by individuals/ homeowners asking for aid, or are you most likely the ones that are contacting businesses, etc., asking to visit and investigate their sites?

They usually contact us. Or they know someone (or meet someone) who is in our group and inquire about us doing an investigation.

The DGHS guidelines offer sound advice, whether you live in the Dayton, Ohio area, or halfway across the globe. "If you feel you are experiencing paranormal activity in your home or at another location, begin by keeping a log of all the activity as to date, time of day, location, witnesses, and description of phenomena," shares Albright. This will help you better assess the situation and, if you choose to contact a ghost investigation group, will provide them with pertinent information, as well. The website for the Dayton Ghost Hunters Society is: www.DaytonGhostHuntersSociety.com.

Chapter 2

A Kettering Ghost Story

Blackie's Mother's House

"I lived in a house in Kettering near Town and Country shopping center from 1981 to 1985 with my divorced mother," says Blackie. The town, named after local inventor Charles Kettering, is part of the Dayton area. "I was in high school when we moved into the house, which was built in 1947."

Blackie knew something was different about this place pretty much from the get go. "From the second night I spent there, I heard the sound of someone walking around the house," she says. "It was not my mother; she was sleeping in the living room, something she did a lot due to back problems. I heard the sound of the wooden floor creaking."

If it wasn't her mother strolling around the house at odd hours of the night, who was it? She had no clue. Those weren't the only phantom sounds that Blackie encountered while at the home, either.

"During high school, I had a friend over one night," Blackie expounds. "We were sitting in the kitchen at the table when we heard what sounded like someone knocking on the window right next to us. It spooked us," she admits. "I looked outside and I could not see anything nor anyone."

Can't Sweep Specters Under the Rug
(or Down the Stairs)

"Over the years, I witnessed strange things," Blackie shares. "One night my mother and I heard the sound of a broom or something fall down the basement stairs, hitting each step on its way down. We did not dare open the door that night and check things out," she admits. "The next day, we opened the basement door to check on the sound we heard the night before, but to our amazement, there was nothing on the floor, and the broom that was hanging up along the side of the staircase was still there!"

What is intriguing about such a scenario is the oddity of what Blackie and her mother both thought they'd heard. It is typical for those who have shared paranormal accounts; something strange that they never imagined happening, happens.

"Even though I have long since moved out, other strange events have continued to happen," Blackie shares, "and actually increased. Although my mom and I can't remember every strange event over the last twenty-seven years, the following are very much remembered."

Music from Long Ago

Blackie goes on to share that one time her mother was sitting in the living room and noticed the sounds of music filtering toward her. "She heard a female voice singing a song about an Indian girl," says Blackie. "She thought it was coming from outside, so she went outside and checked." When she did this, the music stopped.

Her mom then went back inside the house and closed the front door. The woman's singing resumed. "Then she went to the side door and again stepped outside," says Blackie. "But once again the music stopped. She then went back inside the house and shut the side door and the music continued." It wasn't too long after this that the music ceased altogether.

Exploding Tomato

Another episode that is seared in Blackie's mind is a kitchen scenario her mother encountered. "Mom had a trash can in the middle of the kitchen floor," recalls Blackie. "She went into the kitchen and threw away part of a tomato and when she left the room she heard a sound [coming] from the kitchen." Blackie explains that her mother returned to the kitchen to check it out and when she got there, she was startled at what she saw, to say the least. "She looked up and saw part of the tomato on the ceiling, directly above the trash can," says Blackie.

In addition to hearing odd things and viewing the result of their paranormal visitor, Blackie's mother actually witnessed the apparition itself.

"One evening, my mom saw a white wispy-looking thing in the corner of her eye near the fireplace," she shares. "However, when she turned to look at it head on, it was gone."

Not content to merely mess with her fruit, there were other odd happenings in the confines of the kitchen.

"One day my mom came home from the grocery store and laid a loaf of bread she had just purchased from the store onto the top middle part of the stove, where the area is flat and away from the sides of the stove," Blackie says. "She then went into the living room and heard a thump in the kitchen. She walked back into the kitchen and the bread was across the room on the floor in the kitchen, as if it had been thrown."

Hear Them Ring

"In 2007, around 12 pm at night while exercising, the bells she has hanging on her front door started ringing (on their own). There was nothing that could cause them to ring on their own, no vibration from her exercising, and she was laying flat on the floor, not jumping," says Blackie.

Although Blackie and her mother have coexisted with the ghost quite nicely, it doesn't work the same way for Blackie's feline.

"My cat, Rusty, who is very loving and loves my mom, does not like going to her house for visits," says Blackie. "He is very leery of the house, and is always uneasy. When we were over at Mom's house a few months ago with Rusty, I tried to take him in the basement with me where we were using her washing machine for the first time (and the last time, the washing machine didn't work right). Rusty was *very* resistant about going into the basement, and he let out a loud growl, one I don't think I have ever heard him make. I tried to take him down several times with the same result."

Years of strange occurrences have caused Blackie and her mother to wonder what or who is hanging around that house, but they have little to go on in that department.

"We don't know much about the history of the house nor the land," Blackie shares. "Shortly before we moved into the house in September of 1981, the elderly woman who lived there had died, we believe at a hospital. We heard that she had outlived her husband and son. Other than their last name, that is all we know about them."

Today, most of the strange occurrences can best be described as mostly unexplainable noises. "[Mom] has never felt that whatever or whoever it is, is evil," she says. "She is not afraid of it."

Blackie, however, has her own level of uneasiness about the place. "I doubt I would ever spend the night there again unless I had a really good reason to."

Chapter 3

Wright Patterson Air Force Museum

The Wright Patterson Air Force Museum (WPAFM) in Dayton, Ohio, would be well worth a visit, even if it wasn't widely believed to be haunted. Thankfully, however, it is. Dayton is the perfect place for this aviation museum, given the fact that the infamous Orville and Wilbur Wright hail from the area. The history of flight is embedded within this south central Ohio town and is beautifully dictated at this vast museum. Not only is the WPAFM free and open to the public, it is a jaw-dropping example of some of the most amazing machinery that ever took flight from throughout the world. There are also incredibly preserved, touching artifacts from prior eras including the major wars, and the intensity in the exhibits spills forth. Given the emotive components of war and groundbreaking horizons of flight it is no wonder that many believe this place is filled with ghosts.

Exterior of the Wright Patterson Air Force Museum (WPAFM) in Dayton, Ohio.

Over 400 aerospace beauties and many more historical artifacts await your visit (and, likely, some specters, as well). Most are not your run-of-the-mill exhibits, either. Be prepared to see unique and rare offerings that you would be hard pressed to find anywhere else. For those who are not airplane fanatics, by the time you emerge from the massive museum (seventeen acres of indoor museum offerings), you probably will be. At the very least you will find yourself muttering things like, "I never knew that!" and "This was on the moon? Cool!"

The human element is not forgotten here, either. There are several exhibits that tug on your heartstrings and prompt one to contemplate what it must have been like (and still be like) for the men and women of our military to minute-after-minute, put their lives on the line for their country. The POW exhibit is one such example, and yes, it is rumored to be haunted, but there are many more.

The scope of the place can be daunting at first. Massive is not an overstatement when referring to this museum. Allow plenty of time for your visit or you'll be sorry. Take a seat on the bench in front of the *Strawberry Bitch* airplane (don't you love that name?) and see if you can hear its phantom engines revving up. People have claimed that they see movement/life in this crazily-named plane and hear the engines rev.

The airplane was issued in 1943, and was just one of many B-24Ds until it received its pink camouflage paint and, courtesy of its new crew, unique name. The *Bitch* flew in numerous war-time maneuvers, including one where it sustained much gunfire and still was able to sustain flight when several planes around the beauty went down. The plane has had multiple lives, so to speak, and if you ask some folks, they will attest that there is still plenty of action going on in the cockpit of that plane.

Ren'ee Ruble, spiritual advisor from the Dayton area (www.pink-lotus.zoomshare.com), has been to the Air Force Museum multiple times. Each time this intuitive visits, she is not disappointed. "The WPAFB museum is filled with hauntings, noises, and mists," says Ruble. "It's a very energized place, actually."

It seems that there are two definitive areas in the museum that perpetually give Ruble a psychic workout. "My two experiences have been intuitive," says Ruble. "In the plane (*Strawberry Bitch*) I can see the pilot smiling, standing on the platform getting ready to get in the plane. He is very strong with me. I can hear the plane's engine and men celebrating *something* on their return."

Indeed, the *Strawberry Bitch* is one of the most commented upon with regard to visitors hearing or seeing something odd.

The POW Exhibit at Wright Patterson Air Force Museum.

The *Strawberry Bitch* Airplane.

"The Holocaust exhibit makes me very nauseated, and I want to sob there," shares Ruble. "So much sadness fills my being that on most visits, I bypass the exhibit unless a visitor wants to see it. I can hear voices crying asking for food and water... 'Help us', 'help us.' And the smell of death makes me hyperventilate. I just really can't handle that exhibit."

Benches at WPAFM are everywhere so make sure to take a moment or two to rest and gaze upon the exhibits and try and soak it in as best as you can.

It is one of those places that beckons you to return time and time again. Each time, you will notice something new and intriguing. The lights are dim as the museum artifacts tend to like it, and that certainly lends itself to the spookier side of the aeronautical equation.

There are seven galleries to explore beginning with the Early Years Gallery, which, as its name implies, starts at the very beginning, chronicling the origins of flight. The exhibit includes the 1909 Wright Flyer and delves into the impetus and evolution of the Wright Brothers' aircraft on up to America's prepping for WW II. The Air Power Gallery takes over from there, showcasing examples from WWII, including the (haunted?) B-29 *Bockscar*, which is the aircraft that dropped the atomic bomb on Nagasaki, Japan. The *Bockscar*, named after Frederick Bock, the pilot, is an incredible player in the history of the world; it singlehandedly ended a world war. Many died with when the bomb deployed and multiple sightings of a little Asian boy have been seen hanging around this aircraft. The vibe at this plane is all but palpable.

Move on to the Modern Flight Gallery, which scopes the years from the early 1950s to the 1970s. The beginning of the Korean War on through the Vietnam era is covered here.

There are several areas within the vast museum that have been rumored to be paranormally active and it is not only Ruble who has experienced the otherworldly vibes.

"My daughter feels the Nam exhibits," explains Ruble. "She cries a lot when she gets around them. I think she had a past life as a soldier in that war." Ruble's daughter is a psychic like her mother.

I have to admit that this area gave me compelling pause to stop and snap a photograph of a black helicopter, which is included in this book. Peer inside the windows of this copter. What do you see?

The Cold War Gallery follows and holds the 117 stealth fighter, which happens to be the only permanent showing of a B-2 stealth bomber around. Standing below this hovering aircraft is incredible.

Faces peering out from long ago? Helicopter in the 'Nam Exhibit at W.P.A.F.M.

The Missile and Space Gallery, which debuted in 2004 is next and holds a vast assortment of Ballistic Missiles, and at the time we were there, a temporary exhibit of the space collection, including the Apollo 15 capsule. (How nifty is that?)

About a mile from the main museum, visitors will find the Presidential and Research and Development/Flight Test Galleries in a twin-hangar facility. Take a stroll through several impressive presidential aircraft including that of *Air Force One*, the plane that carried President John F. Kennedy's body back to Washington from Dallas, following his assassination on November 22, 1963. This plane was also the locale for the swearing in of Lyndon B. Johnson. Next to this gallery is the Research and Development/Flight Test Gallery housing the museum's experimental aircraft collection. This is where the cool experimental aircraft collection is located. These later two galleries are visited via reservation on a first-come, first-served basis. Highlights include the only remaining North American XB-70 Valkyrie one of the world's most exotic aircraft; the Bell X-1B, a later model of the type in which Chuck Yeager broke the sound barrier; and the only Douglas X-3 Stiletto ever built.

Is there something hanging around the airport hangars at WPAFB?

Keep your eyes and ears open because you never know when you might see shadowy forms move in around the fuselage or perhaps hear a captain snap out an order.

There is plenty to see outdoors at WPAFB Museum grounds as well, aircraft and Memorial Park, which honors those affiliated with the Air-Force and their units for their services to their country. Areas that are off-limits to the public (on the Air Force base) are also believed to be quite actively haunted, as well. Here, however, we will stick to relaying the paranormal activities inside the museum, which is open and readily accessible to all.

Vanessa Penick is a believer. She's heard accounts of phantom sounds and sights from an old friend of hers and his mom who once owned the cleaning company that was hired to work there, and they experienced many odd, unexplainable things. "I have no doubt that they were telling the truth," says Penick.

The area that Penick has difficulties with is the same area that Ruble does. "There is an exhibit that shows what the POWs made while in captivity. When I was standing about 3 ½ feet away from it, I was fine. But as soon as I stepped within 3 feet of it, I began to feel trapped, angry, depressed, scared, hurt, hot, cut, hungry, frightened... all the things that they would have felt," shares Penick. "But when I stepped back to my original spot, I was fine again. To make sure of what I was reacting to, I closed my eyes and had my husband spin me around and then guide me a couple of steps forward. Sure enough, it happened again and when I opened my eyes I was within that three feet. It's as if there is a three-foot perimeter where the ghosts throw their emotions on those who are sensitive."

Cynthia Lee was rather young when she first visited WPAFB museum, but she clearly remembers what she saw and how she felt. "The Early Years (WWI and earlier) gallery, I was all tingly, like all over static. The Air Power (WWII) Gallery was making me seriously dizzy; it was very oppressive in there," Lee recounts from a recent visit. It was her first trip there, however, that was the most profound.

"It was an elementary school field trip, fourth grade, so I was nine/ten," shares Lee. "Don't assume just because I was a kid, I was imagining things (many people have). I was a smart kid, and while fond of myth and fantasy, even young, I knew the difference between reality and fantasy. At the time, I was living in Wilmington; now I live outside Waynesville in Oregonia. My grandfather was a pilot, and my father flies RC sailplanes and worked on a plane while he was in the Navy. The trip to the Air Force museum had me very excited. I was trying to take in every detail I could and I frequently lagged behind the group because I was taking more time to look at the planes. I've found I'm far more likely to see things when I'm feeling energetic or excited.

"About half the displays have mannequins, but it's easy to tell that they're plastic," says Lee. What Lee also witnessed, hanging around the aircraft as a schoolgirl, were beings that were not fashioned from plastic; they looked to be of flesh and blood.

"The one I saw up close was the young man by 'Fat Man' and 'Little Boy,'" says Lee. "Revisiting today, I'm pretty sure they've been rearranged since my last visit, because I'm fairly certain the bombs were in a corner and 'Fat Man' was standing up, and they weren't today. The young man [I saw] had auburn brown hair and was walking away from the bombs," Lee expounds. "He wore a pilot's uniform without a hat. I noticed him because he was on the wrong side of the barriers. He didn't look at me, though, and I had to catch up to the others, so I didn't watch to see where he went.

"Two planes in particular I remember are the C-47 and one of the bombers. The C-47 has a hatch open so you can see into the hold.

I remember seeing people moving about in there. I can't remember which bomber though, because there were three very similar models there, only one didn't have a mannequin in the bubble turret, but during the field trip I saw someone moving about in that turret. The P-51 Mustang also had shadowed movement in it, like someone preparing for takeoff, though that was fairly dim. When my friends finally insisted that there was no one 'real' in the exhibits," shares Lee, "I realized that I really saw something they didn't. It was on the bus ride back home. I'm glad when I get to see ones that don't scare me (there have been a couple who have) but usually I get almost giddy to have gotten to see something that others haven't."

According to Lee, when she told her friends what she'd seen at the museum, they were nonplussed. "They just chalked it up to me being weird again," she shares. "When I told my mom later on, she told me it was because I was gifted and that it ran in my grandpa's family."

Without a doubt, it was that amazing aircraft museum that gave Lee one of her most incredible paranormal experiences of her life. Looking back upon the gift she received, being able to view the ghosts of soldiers from long ago made her feel like she was a part of their world, if only for a moment. "I just assumed they were all part of the exhibit," she says, "until I found out otherwise later."

Even those individuals I interviewed who did not specifically see or hear anything that could be labeled paranormal remarked upon the astounding emotion of the place, and how it evoked so many feelings—from reverence, to sorrow to happiness to awe. Visiting the WPAFM is one high-flyin' adventure, that's for sure.

The Wright Patterson Air Force Museum is open 9 am to 5 pm seven days a week (closed on Thanksgiving, Christmas, and New Year's Day). WPAFM is located at 1100 Spaatz Street Wright-Patterson AFB OH 45433. Admission to the museum is free, but there is a charge for the IMAX Theatre. Web site: www.afmuseum.com.

Chapter 4

Doctor Who?

"My name is Rachel, and do I have a ghost story for you!" This intriguing email landed in my email inbox on a warm spring afternoon and turned into the following true account story.

Although it wasn't just yesterday, Rachel Hunt of Dayton remembers her time spent in the house on the corner of Huffman and Findlay with great clarity.

"My two-year-old son and I moved into a house near downtown Dayton seven years ago," says Hunt. "It was a two-unit home where the upstairs had been refinished into living space and made separate from the downstairs. I was surprised to see that the upstairs unit (the one I rented) had a fireplace and two bedrooms and a cozy kitchen and bath," she shares. Hunter thought she'd hit the renters' jackpot.

The Doctor's House. *Courtesy of Rachel Hunt*

The strangeness began while Hunt was busy spiffying the place up. "I decided to go in late one night to paint the room that was to be my son's room," she says, "and when I entered, I felt like I was being watched." The feeling was so intense that Hunt relays, "I found myself talking to the air and saying things like, 'I just want to make the place prettier,' and 'I hope you don't mind.'"

Odd as it was talking to what she told herself was a seemingly empty room, Hunt continued yapping. "I couldn't help feeling this strange presence and thinking that my painting the room was upsetting this presence," she recalls. "I worked until late in the night and after getting several chills (on a warm August evening), I decided to call it a night and finish during the day!"

Painting completed, Hunt and her son went on with their life in her new digs. "Over the next few weeks we settled in and it started to feel more like a home with every passing day," says Hunt. "One afternoon, I asked my two-year-old son, Trevor, to get his coat from his room because we were going to visit some relatives who lived down the street. I was in the living room when he came shuffling down the hall, somewhat scared, and told me that 'the doctor in the room was looking at him funny.'"

Say Aaah...

Needless to say, this odd proclamation from her toddler came as quite a surprise. "I took a deep breath," she recalls, and said, "'Who was looking at you? Show Mommy.'"

Little Trevor obliged. "He took me to his room and pointed near the window," recalls Hunt. "He said, 'There was a doctor here.'" I picked him up and ran out the door! When we arrived at his great grandmother Judy's house, he was still talking about the doctor," Hunt recalls. "She asked me what was wrong, because I must have looked shaken up. I told her about how I felt in the house that first night and then about what Trevor had witnessed (that day). Judy had been bedridden for about a year, and really didn't know exactly where we had moved to since it had only been a few months after she became ill. She asked me if the house was brick colored with dark shutters," Hunt shares. "She asked me more questions about the house I'd rented and she looked surprised. Judy has lived two streets away on Jersey Avenue for about thirty-five years so I wasn't shocked that she knew what the house looked like. I was scared stiff when she told me that it used to be her doctor's office," says Hunt. "What scared me more is that she told me she would walk down

The second floor window was Hunt's son's room. *Courtesy of Rachel Hunt*

the street to see him every day that she was pregnant with my son's grandmother and that he was the one to deliver her."

Hunt continued to live in the top floor of the house and her curiosity was peaked, big-time. She found herself especially in tune to anything out of the ordinary that occurred.

The Cat's Meow!

"The other strange things that would go on in the house included doors shutting and lights burning out after I had just changed them. The lights can be shrugged off to poor electric," Hunt admits, "and I did keep windows open often because of the warm weather and the breeze could have shut the doors. One night, however, could not be shrugged off by me or my poor cat," Hunt shares.

"It was warm and sticky out so I had my fan on low near my face. I didn't keep the windows open at night because of the area that we lived in (crime was no stranger to this neighborhood), but I awoke with chills all over my body. Then the air turned really warm, and I began to sweat."

Alarmed by this odd turn of events, Hunt was propelled to action. "I went to reach for my fan to turn it up and I realized that I couldn't move my arms," says Hunt. "I tried to sit up but it felt like something heavy was holding me down. I began to panic and started to shift my eyes back and forth around the room trying to see what it was that I was feeling sitting on me. I didn't see anything but I sure felt it! It seemed like it lasted forever, but I am sure that it was only seconds and then my cat, Mr. Lou, meowed loudly and bolted down the hall so fast he smacked right into the adjacent wall. This was amazing considering he was grossly overweight and slept under my bed because he couldn't get his (portly) body on it. As soon as my cat hit the wall, my body vaulted upright so fast I had to stop myself from hitting my face on my feet in front of me."

What is that blob in the second-story window? *Courtesy of Rachel Hunt*

Hunt figures this was probably due to the "force I was building up as I was trying so hard to sit up." But just what was holding her down?

Considering what had occurred, it was not going to be a restful night for Hunt after that. "I grabbed my pillow and blanket and ran to the living room," she says. "I turned on all the lights, TV, and called my friend to tell her what had happened."

As odds would have it, Hunt's stay at what was once her grandmother's doctor's house was short-lived. "I moved out of the house a few weeks later. Not because of the ghost (and more stuff did happen all the time) but because the owner decided she was going to sell the place and not tell me. I only lived in the house for about two months," Hunt adds. "I did drive by the house, recently, and took several pictures of the outside. However, the place is now in the custody of the police department and has been partially boarded up. It really didn't look this poorly when I rented it but it was several years ago and on Huffman Avenue where drugs and crime are now ruining some of the beautiful historic homes in the area."

Although their time in the house was brief, Hunt will never forget those few months on Huffman Avenue. Given the chance, she would love to revisit the home and rekindle her memories there—ironically, to pay a house call to the phantom doctor at large.

Chapter 5

Miamisburg Train Trestle

"If you want to see some ghosts, go hang out at the Great Miami River here in Miamisburg...by the train trestle," Benjamin says. "There have been lots of folks killed there."

(Gee, sounds like a fun place to visit or...maybe not?)

"I've been there by myself," says Benjamin. "I am fearless, but I will not go there at night." Why would this self-admitted macho fellow refuse to visit this site once the sun has set? Seems he has his reasons. He shared one of the major reasons with us.

"My friend and I went for a walk on the bike path there," Benjamin recalls. "It was a calm night and I saw what looked to be a person walking into the woods. Nobody; just branches moving— like a person making way. It kind of freaked us out."

Benjamin went on to say that there were no other leaves rustling or moving at all that night. Just the rustling in that one spot by the Miamisburg Train trestle. It's not just certain sections that spook people out, either. The whole area has a strange, paranormal vibe, notes Benjamin. Even the parking lot.

"When we got back to [my buddy's] truck there was this bottle of water he'd brought still sitting there," Benjamin says. "It was late August, and the water he'd left there was frozen solid."

Odd, yes! How was that possible?

According to Benjamin and his friend, it wasn't possible; at least not by any means that they knew of.

Benjamin advises those who wish to visit the site to bring along an audio recorder and/or a video recorder. "There are these red eyes that you can see from across the river that you can tell blink," he shares. "They move. Yeah, it's possibly animals, but you never know."

True; and you might not want to...

Chapter 6

The Guy That's Haunting Me

Cindy Shaffer and the paranormal have co-existed since she was a child. Odd and sometimes incredible scenarios periodically seep into the cracks and crevices of her life. The most bizarre and perhaps unnerving, however, is what's been going on in the last few years.

Shaffer was acquainted with a woman named Erin for several years before the woman started dating a man named Dave. The relationship become more serious and Shaffer and her husband often did things with Erin and Dave as couples. Sadly after several years, Dave became very ill with liver cancer.

It came to pass, says Shaffer, that Erin and Dave had a falling out. When the couple broke up, Dave stayed incognito at Shaffer's mother's house until he could save up enough money to move to Mississippi and stay with his brother.

"We all became very close," says Shaffer. "He (eventually) did move to Mississippi with his brother, but the whole time he kept writing me and calling me," she adds. "When he got extremely ill, he decided that he wanted to come back here." Once that was decided, "we knew that we had to tell Erin that he was coming back, that he was going to be here [at her mom's], and that he was coming back to die," Shaffer says.

Once again, Dave resided at Shaffer's mother's house where he felt so comfortable and at home. It was while her mother was getting ready to visit Thailand for a month when Dave took a turn for the worse, was admitted to the VA hospital, and then abruptly passed away in May of 2006.

It wasn't long after this middle-aged man's death that the paranormal activity surrounding Shaffer hit the fan.

"He had left me in charge of taking care of everything," says Shaffer. "He had nothing, really, as far as worldly goods. I took care of his funeral and getting his family together and what little bit was left."

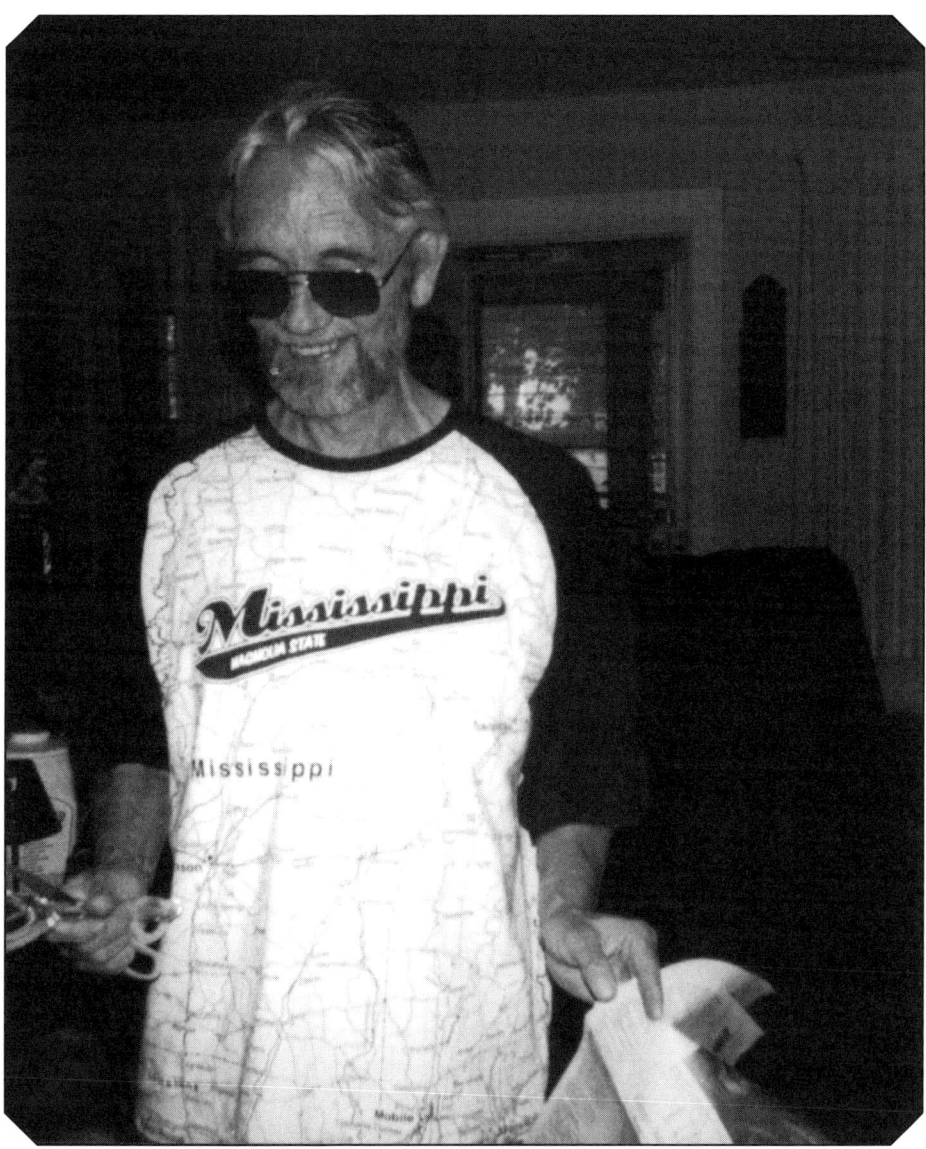

Dave, the man haunting Shaffer, a year before he passed away.

Undying Love...
Taken to a Whole New Level

Shaffer got the shock of her life in the days following Dave's memorial service. "When I was taking his brother, who was from Mississippi, back to the airport after the funeral, he said, 'You know, Dave really loved you.'"

Shaffer automatically responded, "'Well, I really loved him too...'"

"'No...'" Dave's brother said, pausing for emphasis. "'He REALLY loved you ...and I'm supposed to give you this.'"

He handed Shaffer a letter from Dave, a letter that spoke volumes in a few heart-wrenching paragraphs. In the note, Dave not only professed his undying love for her, but also explained that the reason he couldn't tell her what was in his heart was because she was married.

To put it simply, Shaffer was floored. Although there had been small signs of his affection for her here and there during their years of knowing each other, Shaffer says, she truly had no clue as to the depth of Dave's feelings. Feelings that Shaffer makes crystal clear were not reciprocated.

"I'm happily married," she says. "I'm one of those people that actually likes her husband!"

Despite the shock from beyond, Shaffer went on with her usual day-to-day activities upon Dave's passing and life settled back into a normal groove...for a while at least. She started noticing things were awry initially while on the computer.

"I do a lot of *eBay* stuff," says Shaffer, "and I have a *PayPal* account." What's odd is that she soon discovered that, "I'm paying people for (items) and they're sending (my items) to Dave's address with his name on them, in Mississippi." No, she never had Dave's name, address, or any of his info on her account, and yes, it happened more than once. Often, actually. "I've got proof of this," she says.

How odd...but it's explainable, right? Not so, according to Shaffer. "Where my name and address should be, it's his name and address," she adds with an exasperated tone. "I fix it and the next day I look and it's back in his name again." What in the world... (or is it?)

That is not the only paranormal nudge Shaffer has received from Dave, either; not by a long shot. "I have taken his name out of my cell phone," says Shaffer, "and it comes back. I keep getting phone calls from Dave's phone but no one is there. It rings and is just dead."

What is especially chilling is that the phone Dave owned is long gone. "I threw away his cell phone and it still calls me," she says.

Shaffer is a kind, witty, caring woman and it is not surprising that Dave found himself so drawn to her, but she is facing a host of very difficult physical issues herself and the stress of this man haunting her have not helped ease that situation.

"I have diabetes and epilepsy and renal carcinoma of both kidneys and I'm on quite a bit of medication," says Shaffer. "I have this box that I keep my medication in and the other day I found a picture of Dave and his brother that I have never seen before inside." It wasn't there before. Ever. As for how it got there? "I have no clue," she says. She found the photo on New Year's Eve. A Happy New Year from beyond, perhaps?

"I'm always like: 'Get a life, Dave!'" Shaffer shares. "My health isn't that good, I'll be there soon. Give me a break!"

Unlike many who pass over, Dave is not content to send a few signs to his loved ones that he's okay on the other side and be on his way. This fellow does not know when to say when.

According to Shaffer, there is this mechanical stuffed fox that Dave gave to her on Valentine's Day the year before he died. It's a funny little critter: When you press its paw, it sings a song and flashes you, says Shaffer. Well the wily little fox goes off by itself all the time and it is not only Shaffer that pays witness to these "visits," either. "Other people see this stuff going on," shares Shaffer. "My husband says, 'When is Dave going to leave you alone?'"

One night while Shaffer was away, her husband strolled into their bedroom only to find Dave's driver's registration card laying on his wife's pillow. Was it there just a few minutes ago? Nope. He called his wife out of exasperation, but what can Shaffer do to put an end to this?

"I am being haunted by him and I can't figure out what he wants," Shaffer says. "I just don't know what he wants. What does he want me to do? What?" Her frustration is mixed with empathy and fondness. It is a strange situation to be sure.

Shaffer says that recently her husband finally had enough and became very angry at all of Dave's antics from beyond. "He yelled at Dave," says Shaffer, and the mix-ups with the *PayPal* and other accounts have since ceased, she admits. Yet the phone calls still happen, and quite often. "The fox goes off when it wants and photographs appear out of nowhere. I have friends who are with me when this happens and they just think it's the funniest thing in the world that it's happening," says Shaffer.

The woman from southwestern Ohio is not laughing, however. She wishes she knew what is holding Dave around her so closely and wonders what she could or should try to help him move on.

"I just have a feeling that there is something he wants me to do and I don't know what it is," she says. She has her suspicions but isn't sure and is uncomfortable about delving deeper into them. She just wishes Dave would let the worldly issues go and move on.

Yet as far as she can tell, Dave hasn't taken the hint. Once or twice a week he sends a reminder to Shaffer that he is still around and it is driving her crazy; wondering if she is supposed to do something/ find something.

Shaffer talked to Dave's brother, Pat, recently and was quite surprised to hear what he had to say about his brother. "He said Dave is driving him nuts, too," says Shaffer. "He keeps putting Pat's hairbrush in the drawer, when it is supposed to go in a large jar by the sink. This was something that they argued about all the time when Dave was alive and lived with him."

According to Shaffer, that is not the only clue that Pat is getting that his bro is still close by. "He is also getting magazines addressed to Dave, and they are coming to his house...only Pat has moved since Dave died. I guess moving doesn't mean anything to Dave," shares Shaffer. Dave's brother takes it all in stride. "He just cancels the magazines and goes on."

"I think people forget maybe or don't understand even when we don't have our bodies, we retain our personalities when we die," says Shaffer. Although this has been perplexing, weird, and, at times, maddening, Shaffer has great fondness for the man who is reaching out to her from the grave and only wants what is best for everyone involved. She certainly wants Dave to find his own sense of peace, as Shaffer already has. "I have great parents, great children, a great husband; I'm very, very lucky." Hopefully, Dave will find that type of solace soon, as well.

Chapter 7

Stivers Middle School

Stivers School for the Arts in Dayton is filled to overflowing with zeal and energy. Energy from the numerous students, between grades 7 to 12 who attend the hundred year-old school, but if many people are to be believed, energy of those whose physical being has passed on, too. The school is well known throughout the Dayton area for being an incredible place to nurture one's creative side and mind—as well as the site for several hauntings.

Chas. I. Williams, Architect

Stivers Manual Training High School, Dayton, Ohio.

Post Card of Stivers when it was a manual training school a century ago.

First things first: The expansive brick building looks as if it should be haunted from the outset and thankfully it doesn't disappoint. Stivers began its existence as a high school. It was built in 1908, and became a manual training school several years later.

Over its 100-year-course it had several different purposes, including an elementary school and middle school. The Stivers School for the Arts is the most recent incarnation for the site and it is one to be proud of. The school is eclectic, energetic, creation-inducing—with a bit of funky mixed in for good measure. No wonder, as the school is known for its programs in visual arts, music, theater, dance as well as high-quality academics. It is Dayton's only public 7 to 12 grade school, and the only way to get into Stivers is through audition. The majors at the school are a creative kid's dream; encompassing realms such as band, dance, piano, writing, and so much more. Students that attend Stivers have a passion for their majors and must exhibit this passion on a daily basis. Not only does the school employ a top-notch creative staff, but they also have an incredible integration of local and national professional performing artists come by to share their knowledge/talents with the kids—often one-on-one—and the school has regular paranormal visitors. Barrack Obama utilized the school as a campaign stop in July, 2008. (Where was this place when I was going to high school?)

Stivers is a living, breathing building in more ways than one. As their Web site indicates: "Stivers' state report card is similar to that of high-performing suburban schools. Stivers is a prime example of how participation in the Arts enhances academic performance."

J.T. Ryder, a writer and historian of Dayton, used to do alarm responses for a security company in and around his town and he knows Stivers well. "There's a lot of the faculty who will tell you things," says J.T. Ryder. "They have had experiences of electronics turning off and on by themselves and doors unlocking and locking."

Indeed! Sylvia, a longtime employee of Stivers, has had numerous accounts with the unexplained during her lengthy and devoted tenure with the school. "I had no desire to investigate the paranormal or any of that," she shares, "but it wasn't long after I was here that you just start finding things happening to you that you think, 'This isn't objectively something that should be occurring.'" Sylvia smiles slightly. "I had gotten accustomed to things being missing. I would just say, 'Okay this isn't fun anymore...could I please have it returned?' and it would be returned to me."

Actually there have been so many instances of unexplained activity within the walls of that school that it would be impossible to list

J.T. Ryder peers inside the tunnel door where ghost Mary Tyler surprised (and terrified) a visiting adjunct from Japan.

them all in this book. There are several, however, that have stayed put in Sylvia's mind. It is believed that one of the major entities in the school is that of a teacher named Mary Tyler, who many years ago became somehow involved with a boy, who was a senior at the school. Different variations on their relationship flutter about. Her body (completely clothed) was discovered floating in the pool. To add to the mystery, the senior was never seen nor heard from again.

"I'll never forget when I had an adjunct (from Japan)," says Sylvia, "and she was going to be working underneath this office," she gestures downward. "I warned her that she should think about going down there with somebody else." To her surprise, the adjunct found this not only ridiculous, but quite insulting and scolded her.

"I tried to explain to her that there had been multiple sightings of some kind of ghost and apparition below there," says the Stivers employee, "And she said, 'How can you say such a thing? I don't believe those things exist!'"

"I am constantly learning about different cultures and their expectations," Sylvia expounds, and the woman was not about to push

Ever-willing to help, J.T. Ryder descends the ladder into
the shell of the pool where a ghost met her fully-clothed demise.

the point any further lest she insult the visitor from the foreign land. Well, it wasn't an hour that went by, however, when Sylvia found the highly upset adjunct plunked down upon the marble step, quivering against the office door. The woman appeared to be in a state of shock. Sylvia asked if she was okay, but got no response whatsoever. She then made a swipe in front of the adjunct's pale, expressionless face. Still nothing. Finally, she lightly touched the stunned woman's arm. That did the trick; it snapped her out of it, and quick. Her account gushed out.

"'Oh, I go downstairs,'" Sylvia recalls the adjunct saying, "'and all of the sudden, this white ghost, she come towards me! I say, 'stop!' She NO listen! She come closer and go right through me!'" After this harrowing experience, the adjunct never went downstairs again alone. That is not the only paranormal account that Sylvia has been privy to; not by a long shot.

"I have been here early in the morning," Sylvia recounts, "and one morning I saw this young man standing on the stairway with this death grip on the railing." This occurred after the fellow had trotted up the double step of stairs to the elevator platform, she says. Once he was up there, he all of the sudden started screaming. Seems the

Photo of the bowels of the pool now buried beneath a classroom at Stivers. *Courtesy of J.T. Ryder*

boy had seen the ghost levitating in front of him." Sylvia adds that it took two men to get that freaked-out boy's hands peeled off of the railing.

Another time, Sylvia recalls when a fellow employee went downstairs and saw the ghost levitating out of the bathroom down by the boiler room. The woman who witnessed this elevated paranormal show nods in agreement.

Stivers has been widely known as a haunted locale for many years so it's not surprising that a paranormal group visited the site, complete with all of the bells and whistles (paranormal equipment), and they dared to venture down through the tunnel of the school where much of the activity has been noted. Sylvia explains that, back in the day, there were tunnels that connected Stivers to other schools; it runs under Fifth Street. There are seemingly endless underground passageways there. In fact, it was that doorway to the tunnel where the adjunct had her unexpected and unwanted encounter with the resident female ghost: Mary Tyler.

According to Sylvia, the paranormal group's findings were that there was not just one Mary Tyler that's been documented in Ohio haunted history, but there are multiple spirits. The pool itself is purported to be haunted, which is not surprising since it's where they discovered Mary's body. Two years ago, somebody went down and took photos and apparently there is a photograph that shows Mary Tyler there. The pool has been sealed over and classrooms erected atop it, but there is a trap door that leads down to the bowels of the old swimming hole.

There's been so much of it sealed up to try and act like an architectural deterrent to the ghost, says Sylvia, but to no avail; Mary can pass through walls. One night, when a group of prestigious committee members were meeting in the school, Mary(?) started up from down in the lower level with such a tremendous loudness and banging and chains that it drove every member toward the exit.

"They were on top of themselves trying to get out of there," says Sylvia. "It's very threatening," she admits. "I think, too, because we have such an age range of youngsters going through transitions (that adds to the electric environment). It's especially evident in early morning and evening. She really feeds off that energy."

The school has undergone major additions over the past few years but most of them are additions and the original building remains.

"I don't even come down here by myself," says Sylvia, standing by the tunnel entrance. "Only because I don't want to encourage her presence. Yet there are countless people who have to be here at odd times. A teacher encountered her on the Fifth Street Auditorium stage. She presented herself to him on the stage. Another time, we were having auditions here and a teacher and student were up on the fourth floor and she (Mary) attacked him," says Sylvia. "He had another fellow student with him who experienced it at the same time." According to Sylvia, "The student was in such shock that I had to call his parents and they had to come get him because he was unable to carry on. Mary had rushed him and he was in shock. He was holding tears back and then crying." She reiterates the fact that he wasn't a little child, he was a young man.

Wherever you venture in Stivers, it's best to keep in mind that you could happen upon Mary and/or one of the other specters rumored to be in the school. They get around.

"There are multiple places to suspend yourself in this building," says Sylvia. "Sometimes you don't understand paranormal experiences until you've experienced one."

Stivers School for the Arts is located at 1313 E. 5th Street in Dayton, Ohio. Web site: www.stivers.org.

Although recently remodeled, the front view of Stivers has not changed much at all in over a century.

Chapter 8

When the Ghosts Come to You:

Denny Wyburn

"It was in my grandmother's attic in her old Victorian family home in Hudson, Iowa, where I encountered my first full-body apparition," recalls Denny Wyburn. "That apparition turned out to be my grandmother's younger sister who had died in the house from (what was then called) infantile paralysis at the tender age of eight. I was only a child myself," says Wyburn. "I was frequently hospitalized with respiratory problems, and it seemed sort of comforting to me to encounter another child who had made her transition and seemed none the worse for it. It set the course for my attitude and intention regarding investigating the paranormal."

Seems that many a ghost hunter starts early in life; before they even truly comprehend what it means. Wyburn of Montgomery County, Ohio, is a fine example of that. Before Wyburn joined the Dayton Ghost Hunters Society (DGHS) as an investigator in 2007, she had plenty of experiences with the paranormal; from early childhood on up. Of particular importance in her memory is that attic encounter with a loved one that had long ago passed on.

"I was very young—only five or six," recalls Wyburn. "I don't ever remember feeling threatened or frightened. I don't even really remember feeling that it was extraordinary. It just made me curious, sort of like Alice following the White Rabbit. I just wanted to learn more...curiouser and curiouser..."

"[Since that time] I've had a number of personal encounters with the paranormal," says Wyburn. "When I first met the current DGHS president at my workplace, I was actively seeking a group that struck a good balance between skepticism and complete gullibility that would allow me to actively participate in investigations of known activity sites. DGHS seemed to fit that criteria, and I've been very glad that I joined them."

The Residential Center Ghosts

There is a residential facility for developmentally challenged adults in Trotwood, Ohio, which, according to Wyburn, appears to have several residents from beyond.

"The facility itself, part of a chain of ICF/MR care facilities, was built sometime in the 1970s," she notes. "Many of the residents who live there were previously institutionalized in substandard facilities and treated miserably." The residential facility offered a caring, welcoming environment, which was so very much needed.

"For many of them, this facility is 'home' in every sense of the word," Wyburn says. "That being said, I think it's very likely that the entities who haunt the place are there because they feel it is where they belong; they're comfortable there."

Wheelin' and Dealin'

"I believe there were three separate entities; two former residents and a former employee [at the facility]," notes Wyburn. "One of the former residents (a male named Jeff) had used a motorized wheelchair that made a distinctive ratcheting sound, like a child's bicycle with a playing card clothes-pinned to the wheel.

"I had my first encounter with Jeff within a week of starting as Charge Nurse on second shift in spring of 1992," says Wyburn. "I heard the wheelchair coming up behind me, and knowing that we didn't have any residents at that time who had noisy wheelchairs like that, I turned around to see who it was. [Nobody was there] and the noise stopped immediately."

Most of the residents were at workshop, and the only other people in that module were an RA and an ambulatory resident, who also heard the ratcheting wheelchair. According to Wyburn, the duo "had been there a while and seemed to take it for granted."

Seems that Jeff enjoyed tooling around the halls in his phantom wheelchair quite often. "Employees and residents would hear the wheelchair going up and down the corridor where the former resident's room was located," she says, "and sometimes would hear the wheelchair going from the residential area to the dining area or physical therapy room."

Seems that these mechanical, otherworldly sounds were noticed most often on the third shift, but not entirely. Periodically, they would also be noted at alternate times of the day.

People who had been there a while seemed to be quite sure who the phantom wheelchair rider was. "This particular resident had been a very gregarious person in life and was overjoyed when he got his 'special chair' that allowed him to be more mobile," shares Wyburn. "Other residents would talk about him frequently, and not always in the past tense. In fact, on one occasion when I was working second shift, I overheard one of the employees explaining to a current resident that Jeff had crossed over some time ago (about five years previously, from complications of his disabilities) and was no longer here. The resident replied, 'No, he's right over there,' pointing to the door near the dining room. As the employee and I looked in that direction, we all heard Jeff's rackety wheelchair."

Talk about a nifty surprise for Wyburn, but not so nifty for her fellow worker. "The employee, who had only been there two weeks, turned in her notice the following day," she says.

Amiable ghost Jeff, tooling around in his rackety wheelchair. *Courtesy of Sean McHugh*

A Pinch (or Punch) to Make You Flinch

Mobile and amiable Jeff was not the only former resident to stay put at the facility after their physical form had passed on. Wyburn details that "Entity number two (also male) was not so pleasant to be around. 'Paul' (not his real name) had been one of the first residents in the facility, and was a mischievous person with many malicious habits, including teasing the other residents, pulling their hair, pinching them, etc., and then running away, laughing," the DGHS member recounts.

Staying true to his mortal inclinations, "He continued those behaviors on the other side," says Wyburn. "Residents and employees would feel pinches, tugs, and punches when there was no one within touching distance when they were near the former resident's room. When the unwelcome contact had produced a startled response, the victims and others in the area (including myself) would frequently hear chuckling that seemed to fade into the walls."

Getting in One's Hair

Wyburn recalls a favorite antic of the paranormal practical joker. "I had long hair at the time that I wore tucked up in a clip," says the DGHS investigator. "On two occasions, I had the clip pulled on and my hair loosened by invisible fingers."

The ghostly culprit was quite easily figured out, not only due to the behavior patterns, but also by the location of the accounts. "These little annoyances did not seem to occur anywhere else in the building besides near Paul's former room," notes Wyburn.

Poking and prodding unsuspecting residents and employees wasn't Paul's only activity, either. "The window in that room would also open and close, apparently on its own," Wyburn says. "Paul was claustrophobic, and would frequently open the window in his room when he felt too confined. The window was replaced, frame and all, at least once during the four years I was there, but it continued to open and close on its own from time to time. It is my understanding that Paul had died suddenly and unexpectedly from a cerebral aneurysm—but some of the residents and RAs who had been there at the time maintained that he died from orneriness."

Shirley, You're Joking...

The third entity that Wyburn encountered at the residential facility was that of a woman. "'Shirley' was a former employee who had been a Resident Assistant (RA) for a number of years," explains Wyburn. "She had a sad personal history, and a miserable home life, to the extent that she would volunteer for extra shifts because she was happier at work than at home. She died accidentally in a traffic accident while driving to work. Residents who remembered Shirley reported that she came quietly into their rooms at night to check on them. I once walked into a resident's room at night and saw an RA I did not recognize standing at the head of the bed," recalls Wyburn. "I saw her plainly—a plump woman, maybe late thirties or early forties, in light-colored scrubs with curly graying hair held back by a plastic headband and large 'bug eye' glasses. She appeared to be brushing back the hair on the sleeping resident's forehead. I asked if I was on the schedule, and she looked at me directly then, *poof!* she just wasn't there."

During the sighting, Wyburn recalls specific details of the phantom woman. "When she looked at me, I noticed she had one eyelid that drooped and the corner of her mouth was scarred and looked like burn tissue. I reported the incident to the Nursing Supervisor," notes Wyburn, "and she said that the description fit Shirley."

Even though Shirley had long been gone, she made her presence known throughout the facility. "Shirley particularly liked working in the laundry," Wyburn says. So much so, it was like having an extra pair of hands. "RAs who pulled laundry duty reported leaving a table full of unfolded clean linens for a few minutes only to come back to a table full of neatly folded and sorted towels and sheets," Wyburn says. "Soiled laundry would sometimes relocate itself from the gathering bins into the sorting bins unassisted. This helpful spirit so spooked some of the RAs that they would come out to the Nurses Station requesting that they be allowed to leave the door to the laundry room open, or that someone come back and work with them so they wouldn't be there by themselves."

Shirley, the caring
employee who made
the residential center her
home for all eternity.
Courtesy of Sean McHugh

Humming, Helping, Huffing (and Anti-Puffing)

Another means that alerted residents and employees alike to her presence was audible. Seems that while Shirley was alive, she often hummed while performing tasks. "At least twice that I recall, while making rounds on third shift, my accompanying RA and I heard someone humming softly, but could find no source—no other employee or wakeful resident who was making that sound," says Wyburn.

Seems Shirley was a bit of stickler when it came to non-healthy habits, too. "She had also been a militant anti-smoker, and employees taking smoke breaks in designated areas would sometimes find the cigarettes flying out of their hands or lips as if smacked away by an invisible hand," says Wyburn. "A phenomenon I witnessed on more than one occasion, and one that apparently was responsible for convincing some of our smokers to reform."

Way to go, Shirley!

The Community College Ghosts

As indicated previously, Wyburn has had a life filled with a variety of paranormal encounters; many of them that she didn't specifically go looking for. The community college apparition was one such experience.

"I worked for a year as a Grant Secretary at the AIM Center in Building 13 at Sinclair Community College," says Wyburn. "Sinclair, as a whole, is supposedly rife with paranormal activity [Indeed! We cover Blair Hall in the following chapter of this book.], but I can only tell you specifically about Building 13." It was mid-January, 1997, when Wyburn realized that Building 13 held some paranormal surprises.

Joshua

"I worked in an office that was separated from the main hallway by a glass enclosure," she continues. "One evening while closing up, I spotted an older, white-haired man wearing a faded chambray shirt and worn jeans. At first, I thought he was one of the I&M instructors. But I had never seen this guy before and something about him just made the hairs stand up on my neck. Then I noticed that he seemed to have blood on the right sleeve of his shirt. Thinking he might need some help, I watched him as I ran to the glass door of my office, keeping him in sight all the time. When I opened the door to call out to him, he stopped at the top of the stairs and proceeded to just evaporate over a period of a few seconds. Until that time, he was absolutely solid. About this time, one of the security guards came out of the elevator. I told him about the man with the bloody sleeve. He said it was most likely Joshua, one of the resident ghosts in Building 13. I never saw Joshua again while I worked there; however, there were several incidents of doors opening and closing on their own, particularly the doors in the bathroom stalls, and of faucets turning on and off by themselves. I was assured that Joshua was responsible for this activity."

Stubborn as his Mules

"My second encounter in Building 13 took place (in late March 1997) in the basement area," says Wyburn. "There were some reflective partitions in the room. I heard what sounded like someone clicking their tongue, and then two short sharp human whistles (like you'd whistle for a dog) and someone muttering."

What Wyburn then witnessed was straight out of the past. "I looked up to see reflected in one of the partitions in front of me a man in a cap and overalls leading two mules. I only saw about the top half of the man and the mules; the bottom half just didn't seem to be there. I turned around to look behind me, hoping to see the actual apparition, but there was nothing there. When I turned back to look at the reflection again, they had vanished."

After asking some questions, Wyburn learned that, "As the story goes, Joshua was employed at the building when it was the site of the United Color Press. He caught his arm in a press and died from shock and hypoglycemia. Building 13 sits very near some railroad tracks and apparently there was an old roundhouse on the site concurrent with, or prior to, the United Color Press. Mules were used to turn the railroad engines around. During the (Great Miami River) flood of 1913, the mules were trapped in the roundhouse and their wrangler refused to leave them. Mules and man were all drowned. Coincidentally, (or maybe not), the flood of 1913 occurred on March 25-26, 1913, Wyburn adds.

Give Me A Sign

Given Wyburn's rich history with paranormal encounters, it is not surprising to learn her outlook on talking about the subject with others.

"I don't bring it up in general conversation," Wyburn says. "But if I come across someone who indicates an interest, I'm more than happy to discuss it. I'm not someone who worries too much about what other people think of me (in other words, I'm not overly concerned if they think I'm a couple French fries short of a Happy Meal™). I know, after all, what I've experienced: That's my story and I'm stickin' to it."

Wyburn goes on to say, "But I have observed that the subject of paranormal phenomena, especially as it relates to transitioned souls, makes some people very uncomfortable and even downright defensive; so I've learned to be somewhat selective in disclosure."

There are specific signs that alert Wyburn that something paranormal might be going on. "I usually feel a change in the air pressure, sometimes a temperature change, frequently a sort of visual shift in the scene before me like looking through a wave of heat coming off pavement. I know people frequently smell perfume or flowers when spirits are present, but I almost always smell either a sort of after-the-rain ozone-like smell (good spirits) or a sickly-sweet rotting meat smell (bad spirits). Fortunately, there seem to be many more good smells than bad smells."

Given Wyburn's high propensity for zeroing in on "extraordinary" paranormal activities and/or vice-versa, she admits she bears witness (one way or another) to the other side around eight to ten times a year.

These signals do not happen in her current home, however. "If I stay warm and cozy in my own house, I'll never experience anything; the joys of living in a dull, modern housing development," she quips.

"There's absolutely nothing going on here… Well, except around the corner from us in the townhouses where some guy bludgeoned his ex and his stepdaughter to death," she adds. "I haven't personally checked that one out as yet. But some places are like the Haunted Mansion at Disneyland, weird things around every turn."

Wyburn shares the most common signs she witnessed on her initial investigation with DGHS.

"Most of what I experienced there was audio phenomena and the visual shift sensation. Most commonly, I feel atmospheric pressure changes, the visual shift; a sense of displacement/disorientation. I have empathetic reactions to some entities, particularly if strong emotions are involved; I can sort of feel what they feel. Once in awhile I can hear them. When I actually see an entity, it's usually very solid, at least momentarily. But sometimes it's just like a very vivid, vivid memory, which leads me to believe strongly in the residual energy theory, that the universe is one big video recorder and we're all being caught on tape for the amusement of posterity.

"I have every intention of continuing ghost hunting forever, er, in this lifetime, anyway. It's not something I really do consciously, after all. It's just something that sort of seems to fall into my lap from time to time. More than anything, I think it both piques and satisfies my curiosity and my love of learning in general, and reinforces my belief in the continuous circle of life."

Chapter 9

Blair Hall (Hamlet's Haunt)

"I think it's one of the better spaces in Dayton," says Terry Stump, Blair Hall Theatre Manager. Blair Hall, located on what some believe to be quite a haunted campus that makes up Sinclair Community College in Dayton, was christened in honor of Vincent P. Blair, who served as the first Chairman of the Board of Trustees of the college. Blair's leadership and zeal were pivotal in establishing Montgomery County's first public community college. The hall (as have several other campus buildings) has been believed to be haunted almost since its inception.

Blair Theatre on Sinclair Community College Campus

The three-decades-old theater is a proscenium-style arena boasting 459 seats. It is housed along West Fourth Street, within Building 2. The charming venue is the home base of Sinclair's Music Department concerts as well as their Theatre Department productions. It is also used for a variety of purposes (such as conferences, keynote speakers, Holocaust Remembrance, culture programs, political rallies, and other programs for the Miami Valley Community) for the entire Dayton area. Its rich red seats and slanted design provide a feeling of intimacy between the theater-goer and the stage; no matter where they happen to be resting their bones.

Look Out below!

About a decade into its existence, something very odd happened to patrons of Blair Hall. They would be benignly watching the latest play or concert and suddenly be pelted in the noggin from above. Was it the practical jokes of their resident ghosts?

This acoustically-glorious ceiling once rained down hundreds of pellets of wood on unsuspecting patrons (as the glue dried/gave way).

Stump grins widely and shakes his head. "When they put the acoustic ceiling in thirty years ago, they just glued all those 3 x 3 x 2 foot-long wood pieces up there," he says, "and what happened is, when wood dries out it shrinks. About ten years after installation, it started cracking all the glue joints."

The result? Those wood segments acted like little torpedoes raining down upon the unsuspecting patrons. Until the problem was solved with lots and lots of individual screws, the audience was required to sit under the shield of the balcony (or wear hard hats!). Just because that issue has been cleared from the paranormal perspective, doesn't mean odd things don't continue to occur. They certainly do.

Hamlet

Theatre Technology students have hands-on learning by using state-of-the-art stage equipment, memory lighting technology, and the very latest in sound reproduction/recording. These young men and women have been everywhere in that facility from top to bottom and some have seen and heard things that are not easily explained away.

Ally Wetz, a student at the college, has never actually seen "him" whom she rather fondly labels as Hamlet, but says, "Everybody knows the story of Blair Hall ghosts."

"I named him Hamlet because it sounds appropriate to call our ghost Hamlet," says Wetz with a wide grin. "I say goodnight to him every night before I leave Blair Hall."

Wetz, a bubbly, energetic young adult believes she has, however, heard Hamlet—and been a victim of his shenanigans.

"I've been assistant stage managing for the past two quarters here and there's a lot of times I'm alone, backstage and in the dressing rooms and you just hear strange sounds," Wetz says. "There's a thing that goes on in the dressing rooms that they blame on the lights (sensor lights) and they make this weird little beeping sound and sometimes it sounds like a cell phone ring. You can't figure out where it's coming from. The thing is, there's nobody's stuff in there... it's crazy."

Ally Wetz, theater student who named Blair's ghost "Hamlet," being interviewed by Doug Laven.

During a recent production, Wetz and others wonder if the ghost hasn't opted to make his appearance known during the performance. "I shut the cabinet multiple times during the show and it never locks and during our scenes we went to the prop cabinet and it was locked. It was unusual and in concern for the panicked crew. I said, "Hamlet, you're playing tricks on me!" recalls Wetz.

During another production at Blair, recalls Wetz, the catwalk lights came on. Nobody had been up there and they had no idea who or what turned them on. Could it have been Hamlet joining in the crew?

Although Wetz's generation calls the ghost Hamlet, the specter has held other titles. "My tech manager says her generation called the ghost George," says Wetz.

Wetz goes on to say that the most talked about incidents of the ghosts of Blair Hall is that years ago, students claimed to have seen a phantom couple waltzing across the stage. In addition, there is a tale concerning the revolving door out front that has mysteriously started to spin. It has since been locked.

"I [label] him our friendly Blair Hall ghost because he never does anything bad," Wetz continues. "Most of the time nothing happens unless you're in here by yourself." When a person is alone in the venue, sounds are amplified—especially those that don't seem to fit. There are often odd, random noises emanating from the stage.

"This run, I was sitting down here on the stairs, waiting for my stage manager and it kept sounding like these doors [the entrance doors to the theater] were opening and shutting," recalls Wetz. "I stood up and I looked and it sounded like the doors to the hallway were shutting, ever so faint." (However, they were closed and she assumed, as usual, locked).

Theatrical tradition dictates that a single bulb is kept lit on the stage to keep people from blindly wandering off the stage and hurting themselves, but also to ward away potential paranormal visitors. Does it succeed for Blair Hall? Hmmm. Depends upon whom you ask.

As a rule, theaters seem to invite drama of all shapes and forms; including that of the paranormal. The theatrical program at Blair has grown quite a bit in its thirty years and it seems that Hamlet/George has always been around to witness it. The program regularly wins local awards for professional community theaters in the Dayton area, and they are also associated with the Kennedy Center American College theater festival, which is a national organization that promotes excellence in college theater. In fact, Sinclair was one of the first two year colleges to take a show to the regional festival and to the national festival at the Kennedy Center. In recent years, they've made it to the regional festival and won the Golden Hand Truck Award, a competition of all the crews in the festival, which Stump is rightly proud of as they were the first two-year college to win the prestigious prize. It gives one pause: Did Hamlet hitch a ride and help the crew win that night?

Theatrical catwalks seem to be prime targets for paranormal entities to hover around. There are two levels of catwalks at Blair, both sets of which Stump is highly familiar. Yet he has not noticed anything out of the ordinary in his over twelve years as manager. Fortunately for this author, however, others have. The highest catwalk is about forty-eight feet in the air and shows a view of the entire stage.

Former Sinclair College student, Jennifer Kramer, had her own encounter with Hamlet about three-and-a-half years ago up in the black rafters.

"One night I was walking upstairs and once I opened the door to the catwalk I could sense something wasn't right," recalls Kramer. "I walked around the corner and I saw something. Something was

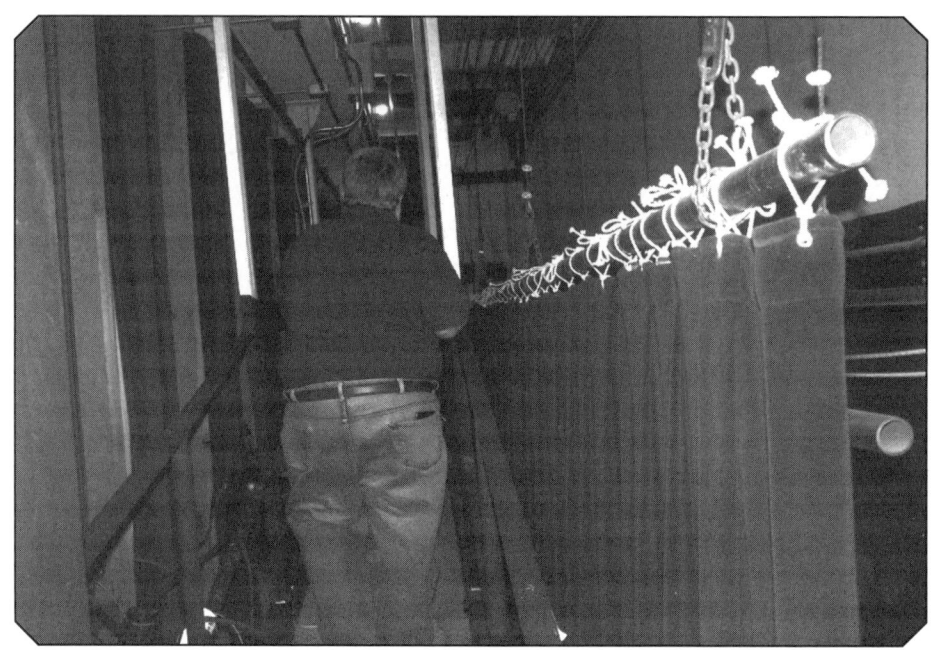

Terry Stump, Blair Hall Theatre Manager traverses one of several (haunted?) catwalks at Blair.

standing there looking at me. It looked like the outline of a person. Tall, slender...but what I really remember was its eyes or what seemed to be looking at me. It wasn't like a person's eyes," she says. "I could just tell it was looking at me. I froze. We stood there for what seemed like forever and then I left. I walked around and went the other way around. I don't remember having any feeling other than to not walk where it was. I knew for some reason I shouldn't walk there that day."

Did She Bring Him Home?

During this same period, Kramer also had an encounter in the upstairs bedroom of her mother's house in Kettering. "On top of this, in my home I saw a ghost," Kramer shares. "I woke one morning, about 5 am, and sat straight up to see a ghost in my room at the foot of my bed. This was involuntary. I never sit straight up. I can't just sit up on my own without using an arm to sit up so I don't know how I did this. But I did this morning. I went from lying down to a ninety-degree angle."

Talk about not believing your eyes! "The ghost in my room looked like the typical white sheet ghost," says Kramer. "It was in the air, no bottom to it. The eyes were not there, it was just black holes. It wasn't a solid figure, I could kind of see through it. I quickly went under my covers and reached out for the remote control to turn on the TV for light. It was pitch black in my room. Once the TV was on, I came from under my covers and went downstairs for a drink of water. Before I could say anything, my mom told me I was white and asked if everything was okay. I told her. She kind of didn't believe me," admits Kramer, "but knew I was white for some reason. I have never slept in the dark again."

Back in the Theatre Where He Belongs

As if that weren't enough to keep her up at night, another paranormal instance occurred for Kramer during one of the theatrical performances at Blair Hall. "I was back stage with other people and we all felt colder than usual. During the production we'd used a lot of dry ice and fog.[It was staged during October 22-30, 2004, *The King Stag* by Carlo Gossi.] One spot on the stage would never have fog or dry ice cover it. It was like a cylinder was placed over the spot and the fog or dry ice just went around it. I was not the only one to see this. We all just looked at it and everyone was astounded by it. They all couldn't believe it was doing this," notes Kramer. (Hamlet does seem to enjoy messing with the lights and props, as any proper theater-housed ghost should.)

If you get the chance, take in a production at the gorgeous Blair Hall Theatre. The students are gifted, the productions are top-notch, the acoustics are grand, and who knows? You might see something unexpected on stage or in the wings, courtesy of their own fun-loving Hamlet.

Blair Hall is located at 444 West Third Street on the campus of Sinclair Community College. Website: www.sinclair.edu/facilities/theater.

According to theatrical tradition, the lone stage light stays lit
to avoid accidents and to help keep the spirits at bay. (What is that in the third
row/balcony?)

Chapter 10

Loved Ones are Never Really Gone

(Candace Allen Perkins)

Losing a beloved family member is one of life's hardest knocks, but unfortunately, we all have to go through it at one time or another. Former Dayton resident, Candace Allen Perkins, remembers the intense pain she experienced in the weeks after her mother's death.

"About six months after she died, I was missing her so very badly, I felt it physically. It hurt that much." There is that moment where, no matter how much faith one might have, we feel a panic—wondering truly if our loved one(s) is okay. What if they're not? Just a flippant thought or fear can cause excruciating agony for those left behind on this earth. Or, in Perkins' case, the finality of the physical departure of her mother was a suffocating heartache.

It often seems that when we reach such a moment in our grief, that is when our loved ones make it a point to show us that they are, indeed, okay (better than okay, usually), and still around us. This occurred for Perkins.

"A song came on the radio that we had both liked (I believe that spirits use music frequently in contacting us, but that is just my opinion)," notes Perkins. "I felt as if we were communicating without so much as a word being spoken, although I'm not sure, because it seemed as if I were in another place. I was driving home from work at the time and wasn't even aware of the physical act of driving, so I'm quite sure God was protecting me. I 'asked' my mom if she was okay, I'm not sure if I spoke the words out loud or in my mind, but suddenly I had the most wonderful sensations going through my body," Perkins shares. "There are no words to describe it. I 'heard' my mom's voice and she answered with one word: 'Yes,' and it sounded musical."

Looking back on her condition and emotions and thoughts from the time, Perkins is in awe. "I'm sure that she was giving me a feeling of what she was feeling," she says. "It was just amazing! I was literally crying and wasn't even aware of it."

Perkins, a teacher who now resides in Nevada indicates that she doesn't believe she was the only one who was paid a comforting family visit from beyond.

"My son also dreamt of my mom," she says. "[He saw her] as a little girl swinging on a swing. I feel she came to him in this manner as to not scare him. He said in his dream he called her grandma, and she responded, 'See Tony, I can run here.' He felt so much better after this dream."

There was another sign that her mom was okay, Perkins believes, one with a retractable head that slowly but surely made its way to their front stoop.

Marty, The "Turtlegram"

"On the day my mom died," adds Perkins, "We had a box turtle just show up outside our door." This was highly unusual to be sure. "To this day, my son swears his grandma sent it to him to help with his grief. We still have 'Marty,' the turtle, and it has been fifteen years. I agree that my mom would have been worried about her grandkids enough to do something like that.

"It is so wonderful to share this very interesting part of my life! The things that occur with an open mind are just sometimes beyond belief. I'm so grateful that I had a mother who taught me how to 'see' things that aren't always apparent to most people and it's a blessing to be able to share this. As we are aware, most people have trouble understanding and I feel so sad for them as they are missing out on some incredible experiences."

The Call From Beyond

"As for other encounters, I have had them with loved ones who have crossed over, including many, many dreams and messages from my first husband, Danny, who died when he was twenty-three," shares Perkins. "He even phoned me several times and many people heard it. I was the only one, though, to actually hear his voice. This was the night of his burial."

Sometimes people think how wonderful it would be if their husband or mother or child who has passed on would somehow be able to phone them/reach them from beyond and let them know they're okay. If it were to honestly happen to many of us, however, the shock and disbelief and fear we might feel could make the scenario not nearly as rosy as we might have originally envisioned it would be.

"I remember my husband's phone calls from the other world as if it were yesterday. My first husband and I had an amazing connection that was also from another time. We didn't have the best marriage (too young), but we were like magnets to one another. Each knowing what the other was up to as if we were physically together even when not. The first phone call came the day of his burial. It was two o'clock in the morning (about the same time in the morning that he had died) and he said, 'Help Me,' as clear as a bell."

Imagine, hearing the phone ring in the middle of the night on the eve of your husband's funeral and he asks for help. Imagine what would run through your mind.

Perkins does not need to imagine this; she lived it, and it was a huge shock to her young system. "I wish every day that I would have been older and more mature to ask what, when, where, how, important questions, but instead I threw the phone. I was in complete terror," she admits. "I will always regret that, but I had just turned twenty-one, and I didn't know the things I now know.

"He was shot to death (which was ruled accidental), but I felt he was murdered," says Perkins. "He showed this to me in the dream, but he never did show whom, or why it had happened, only that he didn't do it himself, that 'someone' had a hand in it. I'm sure he did not want me to pursue it as I had our two-month-old son to raise. I was just a basket case wondering what had happened leading up to his death."

That was not the only call Perkins received from her deceased husband, but it was the clearest. "After the initial call, the times he called after that were so very full of static that if he said anything, I couldn't decipher it," Perkins notes. "Many family members and friends knew that I felt Danny was calling me; therefore I would have them listen to the calls. Each and every one of them said they had never heard anything like it in their lives. Everyone also said it gave them goose bumps, and they as well, felt they were listening to something from another world."

Why did Perkins' husband call her over and over once he'd passed on? She is not certain but has a vague idea. "The calls continued until I got serious with my current husband. I feel, at first, the calls were coming because Danny was confused about his death, then I think he was either checking on us (myself and our son) or he couldn't let go until he realized where he was."

"I think he was trying to convey his confusion at where he was, I'm not sure that he realized at first he had died," she continues. "I felt the confusion each and every phone call. I moved several times after his death changing my phone number several times in the process, yet each time he would call again, even to unlisted numbers; I guess that's not applicable on the other side," shares Perkins. "These calls have since stopped, yet I still do have the occasional dream which is still comforting and usually pertaining to something that may be troubling me at the time. He's been gone for twenty-seven years."

Perkins has been able to move forward and enjoy her life over the years, however, thanks in large part to another, final visit from Danny.

"He came to me in a dream and was beautiful and happy," shares Perkins. "He said, 'Look, Toots, I have everything I've ever wanted here,' and proceeded to show me things that he had 'there' that was important to him here. I think this may be the only way we can understand heaven here. I'm sure it is so much more than stuff but how can one show heaven? And would it be too tempting for us? I mean could we really stand living here if we got a true look at heaven? I'm not sure, but I am 100 percent sure that my husband is there and he is fine, and finally at peace." So is Perkins.

Chapter 11

Mrs. Davis' House... Forever?

"We moved into this home when I was just about to turn fourteen," recalls Diane Jergens of Dayton, Ohio. "My little sister (Candace Allen Perkins) was born two weeks after we moved into that house. It was an older home in East End Dayton."

Jergens lived in the house from the age of thirteen to seventeen, the age she left and got married. Perkins lived there for seventeen years.

According to Jergens, "The lady that lived there before was an odd person (the neighbors told us that). She did strange things like wear white during the night and black during the day when she would go anywhere."

Mrs. Davis' House in Dayton. *Courtesy of Diane Jergens and Candace Allen Perkins*

It seems that this woman did not live an easy life or have an easy death. "Someone had said that she only had one son and he committed suicide in Chicago," Jergens remembers being told. "This lady who lived across the street from us knew Mrs. Davis and said that her body was found at the bottom of the basement stairs three or four days after she'd died." Why or how she fell and, if she was killed instantly or suffered for hours or even days, nobody knows.

"We started seeing things almost from the get-go," says Jergens. "We would be sitting there at the breakfast table and the plants would start swaying. This would happen when there was no breeze, and by a window that was single pane and didn't open." Items swaying in a phantom breeze became so commonplace, it became more the norm than an anomaly. There were other odd accounts, however, that shook the family to the core.

"Right after my sister was born, my mother saw button-up boots tromp up the steps," Jergens notes. "No legs, no body, just boots marching upwards." Not an everyday sight to be sure.

Other interesting things happened in the walls of that Dayton two-story home, as well. One lazy Sunday afternoon when Jergens was a sophomore in high school, the family was sitting around the dining room table when the mixer suddenly burst on. "We thought there was a power surge or something," recalls Jergens. Her dad told her to go shut it off and Jergens vividly recalls that the minute she walked into the kitchen doorway the mixer suddenly stopped, just as suddenly as it had started. What's even more astonishing is that when Jergens walked across the linoleum to investigate, she saw that the mixer had never been plugged in.

Dumbfounded, she returned to the dining room and sat back down. Thinking his daughter had been the one to turn it off, her dad asked her if she'd unplugged it so that there wouldn't be a mixer-blasting encore. She informed him that there was no need to do so since it had never been plugged in, in the first place. Somehow, the family wrote this off, too, and went on with their daily lives.

Jergens' brother had his own odd experiences in the house, to be sure. "He was five years older than me," recalls Jergens, and he came into the house one day (and saw Mom in the dining room); as he strolled into the kitchen he saw her again (?) standing at the sink, doing dishes. 'How did you get in here so fast?' he asked his mother. She had no clue what he was referring to since she'd been doing dishes the whole time he was there. Her brother, however, was adamant that he had seen their mother, plain as day, in the dining room.

Another time, when the children were adults, Jergens' parents were gone one day, and her brother stopped by (they never locked the door) and he heard what sounded like a professional wrestling match upstairs. *Crash, boom, bam!* Knowing that no family members were present (nobody living, anyway), he hightailed it out of there. He never went back to the house when he knew he'd be alone again, says Jergens.

One of the most profound paranormal events happened to the youngest of the Jergens clan. "When my sister was about four," recalls Jergens, "she had an experience that was incredible." To be sure, the amazing event is seared into Candace Allen Perkins brain.

"When I was four, I saw Mrs. Davis (in my brother's room)," says Perkins. "I wasn't scared or threatened by her. I was startled, because I realized even at that young age she wasn't supposed to be there. She was just looking at me through glasses, which were low on her nose. Her dress and shoes were that of a different era."

Perkins shares that she was obviously curious as to who this older lady was and what the heck she was doing in her brother's bedroom. The two females of markedly different ages (and eras) stared at each other for a few moments and then reality settled in for Perkins. It dawned on her that this was definitely not a normal visitor.

"I yelled for my mom," recalls Perkins, "and she came to get me but the door was locked from the outside. It was an old eye and hook latch that I couldn't have possibly reached."

Despite this occurrence, or perhaps because of it, Perkins holds a fondness for that specter of a woman to this day. "I really think that Mrs. Davis liked me, and I felt a kind of kindred spirit thing with her. Later on, when I was about eleven, a medium came and supported my feelings by stating that Mrs. Davis looked upon me as a daughter she'd always wanted."

Her sister simply did not hold the same fondness for the house, or the woman specter occupying it, however. "A lot of times throughout the years when I was coming down the stairs, I would feel like somebody was behind me," says Jergens. "I would hurry down the steps because I didn't want somebody to push me down." The uneasiness and mild fear was extremely unnerving for the then-young adult.

The paranormal experiences, courtesy of Mrs. Davis, did not cease for Jergens once she become older and moved out of the old woman's former (?) home. "When I was about thirty, I was going to visit Mom and Dad, and the door was unlocked and they were gone. I walked in the door," she recalls, "and noticed something was odd because the dog, Boots, didn't run to greet me. I went through the foyer and I was standing in the doorway to the living room and Boots was sitting on the end of an end table, looking out the bay window. I remember thinking how strange that was," notes Jergens. "She usually comes up and greets you. You know, at least barks or something. And she never sat on the end of the end table, either."

Perplexed but intrigued, Jergens, having lived in this haunted home for many years, couldn't help but instinctively wonder if the dearly departed former owner didn't have a hand in Boots' strange behavior.

Jergens made her way over to the pooch and chuckled. When she was about four feet behind the dog, she spoke. "If you're really Mrs. Davis, raise your right paw." Jergens laughs. "I can't believe I said it, but I was just kidding around." What happened next was priceless.

Slowly, and quite robotic-like, the canine craned its furry head in her direction and then, almost unbelievably, waved her right paw at Jergens. Whoa... the shocked woman could scarcely believe what her eyes had just witnessed.

"I backed up and ran out of there," says Jergens. "I never knew if she stayed in the window after that or not." Although she understood that it was incredible to believe, she was compelled to tell her family what their family pet had done. "My dad would tell that story (to outsiders) and I would say, 'Dad don't tell that story! (People will think I'm nuts.)'"

"Over the next few years, my dad repeatedly asked me, why would you even ask the dog a question like that?" says Jergens with a laugh. "I told him I was trying to be funny! I was just joking around." She admits that she wasn't laughing as she raced from the house that day, that's for sure.

Although there were some lighthearted moments in the mix, life for Jergens in that house was a challenge pretty much from day one. She shares that her father had been an alcoholic who had abused her as a child; yet she is very grateful for one thing. One day, while she was an adult, she and her father were sitting at the kitchen table, waiting for her mother to come downstairs. That day he took it upon himself to apologize to his daughter for hurting her. It was just a sentence or two but it was immensely healing to Jergens. She was able to forgive him (a prime example of the type of individual this woman is). His admission and apology, and her forgiveness gave her closure. She is especially grateful for that moment in time because when the warm, kind woman was in her early thirties, her father committed suicide in that house.

"He was downstairs in the basement and he shot himself with a 38," says Jergens. "My dad was still alive when we found him. I went down there and stayed with him until the ambulance came." Coping with that memory has been a lesson for Jergens. "You just put it in perspective and you learn from that."

In 2007, Jergens and her sister, Perkins, who was visiting from Las Vegas, made a trip to their old homestead. The fact that it is located in a neighborhood that has deteriorated greatly (crack houses line the street) is difficult for Perkins to fathom. Her connection to the house is one of affection; whereas Jergens sees it more along the lines that she learned how to swim, not sink there.

The sisters reentered the place that was filled with so many intense memories and started up the stairway. They roamed around in their parents' old bedroom and suddenly both of them remarked, at the same time: "I can't breathe…"

The siblings felt severely oppressed, recalls Jergens. They went back downstairs and the photos they snapped at that time showed multiple orbs, but much more importantly, blobs of energies. The interesting point is that these were taken in rapid succession yet some were clear and others were all but filled with what appears to be ecto mist. The ecto was shot mostly in the living room and the dining room.

The sisters returned to the home the next night and Perkins went back into the basement, but Jergens did not. "I still had that image (of his suicide) in my head," she says. She had gone down there the night before and told her sister she didn't want to go back down there again even though she admits that the first night had been uneventful. "I didn't feel anything strange down there, which was kind of surprising," says Jergens. Still she didn't want to press her luck.

While her sister was in the basement that second night, however, Jergens was standing in the kitchen waiting and all of the sudden she says she felt kind of strange. The same kind of feeling that she'd experienced in her parents' bedroom, but not quite as strong. Her sister took a photo of her there in the kitchen with her arm on her chest, and there is an orb perched above her head.

It was not just family members who felt something odd was going on in that Dayton house. Perkins' best friend lived right in back of them; their yards abutted. Her friend still owns the house and currently rents it out. In doing so, she has kept up on the history of the old home. She told them that the last people who lived there were a military wife and her two little boys.

The house is void of living inhabitants. *Courtesy of Diane Jergens and Candace Allen Perkins*

A room filled with ecto. *Courtesy of Diane Jergens and Candace Allen Perkins*

One day, the woman came to her and told her, "I'm moving. I can't stay in that house." Turns out the woman and her boys experienced multiple strange things there; most notably in the basement. Seems that she would think somebody was breaking into the basement and she would call the police and they would come but would find nobody down there. The woman also had made a playroom in the basement for the little boys and one day, one of her children came racing upstairs, crying hysterically. After calming down a bit, he told his mother that a man wearing a sweatshirt and jeans was down there; and that he was covered in blood. This woman had no clue that Mrs. Davis had expired, laying for days at the bottom of the basement steps, nor that Jergens' father had committed suicide down there (and that the despondent man was wearing a sweatshirt and jeans at the time).

"I have always known that spirits are among us and have felt their presence many times over the course of my years here," says Perkins. "Actually seeing Mrs. Davis is right up there in the top, but always unexplained things would occur."

Perkins recalls the mixer incident and her mother's sighting of the phantom shoes. "I personally thought it was funny when many people were so afraid of my home," she says. "Many people hated

What...or who is this swirling mass of mist in the living room? *Courtesy of Diane Jergens and Candace Allen Perkins*

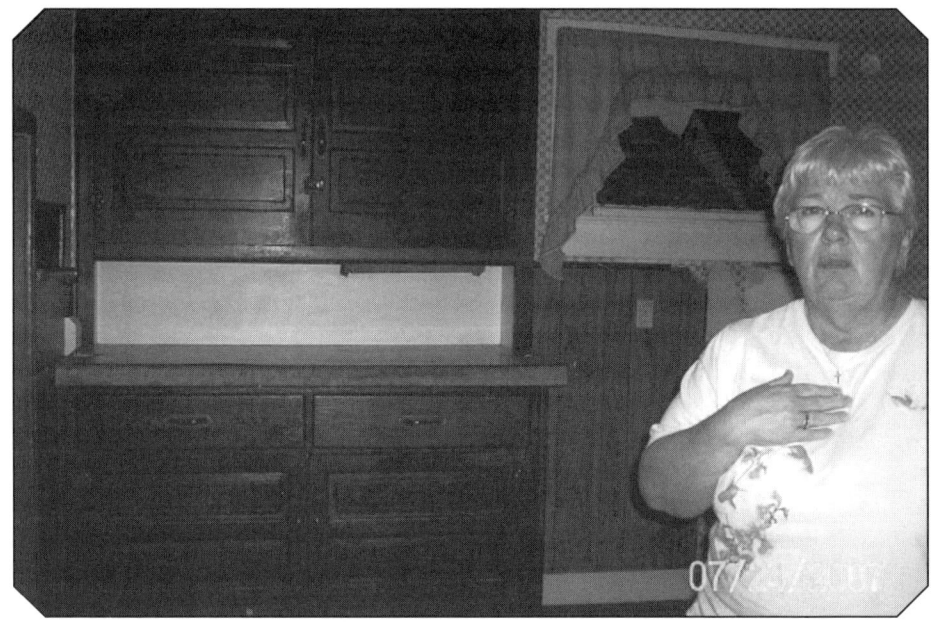

Diane Jergens in the kitchen of her old home. *Courtesy of Diane Jergens and Candace Allen Perkins*

The basement (where two people died). *Courtesy of Diane Jergens and Candace Allen Perkins*

to even come in. My best friend still won't look toward the house when she is in the neighborhood."

"When we retain an open mind to childhood experiences I'm sure that we could all experience more. Thankfully, for me, I have, and have wonderful encounters from spirits through encounters and dreams. The messages are always comforting. God would not allow negative spirits to enter our lives, this is why I'm not afraid. I trust in God to keep me protected, always."

"I think for some reason Mrs. Davis is still there, because I felt her again when my sister and I entered the house this past year. I don't understand why she doesn't move on, or if she has and her energy is just so strong. I felt others, but I haven't a clue who they may be."

When all is said and done, it appears that old Mrs. Davis' house remains Mrs. Davis' house; all those many years after her death.

Chapter 12

If Homes Could Cry

"Why am I talking to you?" Sallie queries me. "Maybe you are my sounding board for these hauntings. I hope that's okay. I should be working. I own a business, but we are slow. Good excuse, I guess."

Sallie's intense connection with this house is readily apparent. "The house is sad. Very sad, that house. The house makes one want to cry, like mourning a loved one," she adds. No doubt that this house on State Route 571 in Yellow Springs is haunted, according to the middle-aged business owner from the area. "It was pulled up in the hill—on 571, by the Miller Brothers Construction back during the horse and buggy times. It used to come from an old mill. People lived, died, and gave birth in this house. I lived in this house for about four years (and moved out three years ago). It has been added on many times throughout the years," she notes. "This house has ghosts, issues. They are friendly to me, but not to my daughter, who lives in San Diego now.

"When we lived there, my daughter was scared," admits Sallie. "I told her I thought that the house might have ghosts, but that they are happy. Now I'm not so sure. I never felt a bad feeling until I entered the upstairs where her bedroom was. It is really a sad room. She was always scared back then, but I blew it off as a childhood thing.

"When I moved out in 2004, my then ex-boyfriend, Burt was still living there. He said that things started getting active," she says. "I laughed because I knew they did," she admits. "I likely wished this on him because I was emotionally hurt. It makes sense.

"After I left him (about six months) passed, and he called me and said, 'Tell them to just STOP!' He thought I had something to do with the ghost. I might have," Sallie admits. "I was very angry, to say the least, and did some things to possibly help Burt's fears become known to him. Now I'm not so sure I had anything to do with it. I have a history of picking up on BAD ghosts and not so much good ones. The good ones I do come in contact with I relate to my grandmother being with me. She died at 105 years. We were very close. I talk to her when I'm scared....make sense?"

Suffice to say, the paranormal residents of the house were not kind to Sallie's boyfriend. He still lives there, she says, adding that she will stay the night in the house probably twice a week (they are now back together). "We are in our forties and fifties," says Sallie, "we are not kids. I am a professional business person; I own a few businesses and was in the Navy." These impressive facts don't seem to matter to the visitors from beyond, however.

Burt has even been known to sleep with a pistol, due to the hauntings. "Last night, I was there, it was about ten-ish and we both heard something," she recalls. "He jumps up. I am ALWAYS the calm one and I try to pass everything off as anything but a ghost," Sallie says. "I do this for his sake, but I often wonder," she admits. "We jockey back and forth about trying to explain away the occurrences. You must realize, we are older and have been in some 'real' scary situations in life." Many people will agree that reality is very frightening on its own, let alone when you toss in a ghost or two.

"We have never had an investigation into the hauntings in Miami County," she says, mainly because her boyfriend believes that if they acknowledge the specters in that manner, it will only serve to encourage them, which could likely make their antics grow more obtrusive and commonplace.

"I tune out any notion of a ghost when I am at the house now," says Sallie. "If I don't do this, I can't relax. I often wonder what would happen if I tuned in. I do know that I would have a hard time being alone in the house now. I didn't used to feel this way."

It seems that once Sallie left the premises three years ago, things shifted, and whereas before she felt she was "in charge" when she lived there 24-7, it is no longer the case.

Showered with Practical Jokes

Burt could not take a shower for many months without hearing loud banging upstairs on the walls, notes Sallie, adding that, no, it's not the home's water pipes. During the first few times this occurred, Burt would put on a robe and go to the front door. Nobody was ever there. Once he stepped out of the shower and put on that robe, the banging would stop. The minute he'd remove the robe and step back into the shower, the banging would start again. It seems these antics have lessened in the last months, but Sallie is not completely sure because Burt, "Doesn't share these things much of the time. Probably due to the fact," says Sallie, "if we voice it, it's real."

A Phantom Click of the Switch

Another common occurrence has to do with electricity. "He would turn the wall light switch off," says Sallie, "and it would turn on by itself right after he went back and sat down. Not just the light, but the switch also.

"He hears the voices very often, especially in the front room, when he is alone. We don't talk about it much," she admits. Turns out the voices are one of the most commonly noticed anomalies in that Yellow Springs abode.

"We even hear voices together," says Sallie. "Like a crowd of people talking all at once. A very modern sounding crowd. I don't know why I say that," she admits. "I'll say, 'Honey, is the TV on?' and he'll respond by saying, 'No, but you do hear them don't you?'

"The voices are coming from (at least to me) right next to my head or close, I guess. It's rather like a little old transistor radio is in my head. They' are talking fast," Sallie says. "I hear women and men, too, but it is mostly females. It's not a frightening conversation; it appears to always be a room full of people, like they are having a meeting."

What is particularly perplexing to this ex-servicewoman and business owner is that the voices correlate with something completely unexpected. "I hear their voices in color, their speech is blue, white, black, and shiny like silver. Can we hear color?" she asks.

That's something most people have probably not thought about, but it is intriguing, nonetheless. According to Sallie the voices are most noticeable right when the couple goes to bed. "We listen to the house," she says, "but neither one of us will focus on this for very long, and we snicker and try to sleep."

"This is going to sound crazy," Sallie adds. "How about seeing tubes? Long, long tubes. Tubes about five inches in diameter and as long as a room is wide appearing, and actually extending, then fading into themselves. Have you ever heard of these tubes? They scare me. They are accompanied by a noise. A sound like coins being dropped by the hundreds, very fast. High pitched. Oh, and these tubes bend. Does this sound crazy? Ever had anyone mention tubes? Here's the weird part: Please don't think I am a nut case. I have seen them come out of the walls up by the ceiling and bend down toward me, only to fade away a few inches from my body. I am frozen with fear when this happens. It sounds silly when I (talk about) it."

Sallie wonders repeatedly why she opted to contact me. "After I (shared my accounts with you) I thought to myself, 'What the heck am I doing telling a *stranger* these things?' This is very personal." The word cathartic comes up during our exchange and seems to fit the bill.

"My boyfriend has these experiences very often at his house. He is very 'jumpy' in his own home—especially once I moved out.

"When I am not there, Burt's big recliner will rock by itself," she shares. "The TV will turn on and off. The lights will go on in the front room, the upstairs door will open. The house is old. It is settling and creaking for sure, but lights do not turn on and off by themselves. Even outside around the house is spooky. It does not look like an old spooky house, it just IS.

"I'm getting chills (sharing) this," Sallie notes. "In the past Burt became really freaked out, then as time passed, he got mad at 'them' and told them to STOP bugging him. He will talk to them but do they listen? Who knows?

"I tell Burt that everything is okay. I protect him. He lives there; I do not. Only this morning (Burt had left for work), I failed to open a bedroom door and look for a shirt because I got creeped out. I stopped in my tracks, did not hold the doorknob, went no further. Turned around and got mad that they were doing this to me again. I hesitated taking a shower because I was alone. This always makes me angry: when they make me scared. I get mad."

The entire house can be the locale of a paranormal encounter, but it is the lowest level that seems to elicit the most dread. "I have lots of my personal items stored in his basement. When I'm there we talk about going through these things, but we never do. I guess we are silently telling each other that we don't want to go in the basement. We will never admit this to each other," says Sallie.

"Burt thinks I have control over these hauntings," writes Sallie. "Do I?"

That's a very good question.

Chapter 13

Oxford Motorcycle Ghost

Life can be at its most cruel when we are poised highest atop the peak of happiness. An example of this notion concerns a local legend swirling around Miami University, in Oxford. It centers upon the tale of an excited and enamored Oxford, Ohio, man. Seems this young fellow was wildly revved up to propose marriage to his beloved girl. So revved up, he hopped upon his motorcycle one fateful night and zoomed off to her home in order to ask her for her hand in marriage (and, assuredly, the rest of her, too). It is said that the young man and his lady had a "signal" they used to let each other know they were there (seems like her parents might not have been so thrilled about this young coupling). He would flash his headlight three times and wait for her to come meet him.

In his zeal to reach her as fast as possible, he came barreling down, far too quickly, upon her street, which was located on a private residential drive (at the corner of Oxford-Milford Roads). Unable to maneuver the abrupt turn into her driveway, he slammed into a barbed wire fence at full speed, a tragic and bloody accident, which resulted in his untimely death.

Some Miami University students believe that even though this happened many years prior, this fellow, although deceased, has not abandoned his efforts to finish what he started; he remains determined to propose to his beloved. Many students and ghost hunters alike, have taken that same route at night, in an effort to witness those telltale lights, presumably elicited by the ghost of this fellow.

They drive to the area and wait, facing south, in the driveway of the house where they believe his intended once resided. In a precise ritual, they flash their car headlight three times in a row, which results in what many have claimed to be the telltale single headlight and tailgate lights shining back at them.

It is asserted that the light could not possibly be from another vehicle, since those lights also illuminate the sky and surrounding foliage. The "summoned" light is always beamed straight ahead.

The Oxford Motorcycle Ghost.
Courtesy of Sean McHugh

Residents who have lived in the area for many years, however, say they do not recall ever hearing anything about such a horrific accident occurring, but one local fellow went on record with Mark Spencer of the *Hamilton Journal-News* as saying, "They (students and ghost hunters) wouldn't come out here if they didn't see something."

This particular fellow admits that he is inclined to think there is something unexplainable (supernatural) happening, but his hypothesis is that the activity stems from Indian burial grounds, which are located in the area where he believes might have been disturbed.

This neighbor's reasoning makes sense because it truly does appear that people are often seeing "something" unusual/unexplainable at this site. If they didn't, the legend would likely fade into the Ohio mist. There are other scenarios about the Oxford cyclist, as well, but regardless, they all end up showcasing that telltale, single white light.

Another rumination on the story has to do with Buckley Road (or, depending upon whom you ask, perhaps Route 732) in Oxford, where it's said that a bicyclist was hit and killed by a car or a motorcyclist (the same enamored young man, perhaps?) who was coming to meet his girlfriend after she'd done their "three light" signal.

Legend has it that this bicyclist continues to traverse the roadways there upon his bike and you will see an indication of this if you turn down Buckley Road, (out of the town of Oxford) and drive until you come to the curve in the road. Then you should make a u-turn and face the route you just drove in on (Route 732).

According to legend, the car's engine should be turned off, and again, just like above, flash the vehicle's headlights a total of three times, you will eventually witness something coming toward you from the direction of the hilltops. That "something" is a single white light.

Self-described urban legend history investigator, Alex Scales, had an incredible experience at the Milford Oxford site and has written about it. He admitted that what occurred on that rural stretch of roadway was "probably the weirdest thing to ever happen to me."

Scales is an Ohio resident and notes that Ohio is chock-full of ghost stories and urban legends. He's spent the last several years researching them and documenting them. According to Scales, southwestern Ohio's most told story is the Oxford story, the one relating to that mysterious light.

"It's the most clichéd story ever told," admits Scales, "and I've heard several variations of it from all over the country." He adds, "It's especially hard for me to take this story seriously since it comes straight from a college town, which are full of shenanigans!"

Scales admits that he has visited the site numerous times, and for the entire first year, he was in the wrong place. He ultimately found the right place in the road (in front of a house that still stands), and armed with a video recorder and walkie-talkies, he and a group of friends flashed their lights three times.

"Sure enough, and much to my disbelief, there it was," writes Scales. "A single, bluish-white light seemed to actually make its way down the road." Scales indicated that he mistook it for a car, but soon ascertained that it wasn't a car.

Instead, they watched the light at the top of a hill fade in and out without ever coming down toward the young men. According to a friend of Scales, "It looked like it was underwater."

The urban legend aficionados then rode up the road in the direction of the light and found there was nothing there. They turned back and tried again; this time parking in a driveway. They were shocked to see that before they'd even flicked their headlights, or for that matter, turned off their engine, the light was "already shining back at us. The light was incredibly bright," writes Scales. It was so bright they wondered if the light was a reflection from cars coming down the road. That theory was debunked when Scales got out of the car. He looked way down the road and saw truck lights. He said nothing, waiting for his friend to say he saw the light, but he "saw nothing but darkness."

The approaching car's light, nor the reflection theory were the answer. The men then drove around looking for any clues they could find; anything to give them some answers. The pair realized after a while that a "car" that was behind them appeared to have that same "watery glow." They pulled to the side of the road; their eyes glued to the wavering orb. This light, too, faded in and out, noted Scales "and seemed to hover brightly about a yard away from us."

At about this same time, Scales realized that he was seeing more than one light; in addition to the bluish, white light, there was a blinking yellow light. "Like a turning signal!" wrote Scales. "It was like it followed us for the whole time."

According to Scales research, a librarian at Miami University in Oxford has a file filled with people's accounts of witnessing that same light, but the origins of the story/ghost remain just as fuzzy as the light, because, again, no records exist of a motorcycle crash. Scales has a DVD–R that has footage of the light that he plans on putting on his website for others to see. Web site: http://www.alex-anderscales.com/.

Chapter 14

A Family of Psychics, Naturally

"I guess it is kind of phenomenal but we have just always been surrounded by it, and I have never questioned it," says Carol from Liberty Township (Dayton-area), Ohio. "My mother and brother are psychic, as well," she adds.

"My house, built in 1999, is truly an interesting place, but I attribute that to us as a family. I think we draw this stuff; I might be a catalyst." There does appear to be some connection between certain individuals attracting the attentions of those that have passed on. Being psychic is one of the most common attributes for this.

Interestingly, sometimes people have a preconceived idea about what a psychic should and/or does look like. Perhaps they envision these elusive intuitives clad in long, flowing, flowery robes and bedecked in shimmering crystals from wrists to ears. Certainly there are psychics who do adopt that attire and adornments, just as there are many others who do not; like Carol.

This soft-spoken, well-educated professional woman and her well-to-do family live in Liberty Township, and neither Carol nor her family look as though they were poised to predict the future. Instead, the clan appears just as any family might; say, while sitting down for a meal at the local eatery. Save for the fact that while they are waiting for their chicken fingers to come, her children will pass the time by not drawing on the back of the menu, but instead, honing in (with a high degree of accuracy) on which color of crayon their father is hiding under the table. This is all natural to Carol who comes from a family of psychics from the Salem, Massachusetts, area. After all, if you can't be comfortable with your paranormal gifts there, where can you be?

Years ago, Carol moved to Ohio with her husband and their two psychic children. Turns out, the only person in the household without psychic abilities is Carol's husband. He's become accustomed to being the odd man out in this faction. It took some time, admittedly, for her husband to grasp the full potential of his wife's gifts.

"I would say things to my husband like, 'Get in the left lane there's going to be a car accident up there,'" recalls Carol. At first her husband would not be readily inclined to believe her, but after five or six times of witnessing his wife's accuracy in her dire predictions of what was waiting at the bend in the road, he eventually learned to switch lanes without question.

The onset of her abilities came as a child. At the age of about thirteen, Carol remembers having her dreams come true; however, this was with the exception that one facet of each dream would not be right.

One particularly vivid and distressing dream, for example, involved Carol vacationing on Cape Cod and walking over the face of a person who had been eaten by a shark. The next day on the beach, she walked over the face of a shark that had been torn when cut up for fishing.

"When I was real little," says Carol, "I dreamt that the family got a black and white cat. The next day we got a black and white dog." Carol stresses that, prior to this, the family had not ever discussed adopting any sort of pet at all. It came out of the blue.

As indicated before, Carol's young daughter and son are both gifted with a special sight; but it is her five-year-old boy who seems to have inherited the bulk of it.

"I got the feeling that my son would be strong with it when I was pregnant with him," says Carol. "I was told I'd have my baby on May 25 and I said, 'No, it will be May 1.'" She had the ultrasound technician write her prediction down and, indeed, she delivered on that day. She also knew something important would happen on July 7. From the time she was small she felt that something "was supposed to happen" on July 7. Indeed. Her daughter was born on that day.

Being raised in a household where it was understood that there were psychics in the family helped Carol cope with the manifestations of her gift from an early age. She is, however, concerned with what those in the Dayton-area of Ohio would think if they knew she and, especially her children, were so psychic.

"My biggest fear is that they will be seen as freaks," says Carol. "Otherwise, it's never bothered me."

For example, her son's prowess with precognition has already all but alarmed his preschool teachers. His uncanny ability to "know" precisely when his mother was stopping by the center unnerved them to no end. Out of the blue, his mom might get a free moment and decide to drive over there with no warning and several minutes prior to her arrival the boy would go and stand by the door, waiting to greet her (to the shock of the unknowing preschool staff).

Happenings such as this culminated in a meeting between preschool and family, urgently called by the teachers. When they voiced their concerns over her son's ability to sense when things would happen, Carol having no choice, told them about the family and their history with psychic ability. If they weren't going to be okay with that, she says, "then I would have had to move him to another preschool."

She utters a slight laugh. "There were some wide eyes," she admits, "but really, the teachers pretty much just said, 'Okay, that explains a lot.'"

Her son is also gifted intellectually, and when he went for testing for that, Carol was surprised when a representative of the gifted program in the school system flat-out asked if he was psychic. "'We very often find that gifted students are psychic, too,'" the school district representative told the Liberty Township mom.

Although Carol knew she was psychic at an early age, she finds that her son is discovering his gifts earlier than she did and with better clarity right out of the gate. "He seems to see more depth than I did as a child," says Carol. "For example, we went to put flowers on the grave of a fallen soldier (who'd been their neighbor) at Arlington Cemetery when he was three," recalls Carol. Her son was barely out of the car when he had a pronounced reaction and aversion to the locale. "'You've gotta get me out of here!'" he told his family. "'There are soldiers all over the place and they're (upset!).'" This made her usually calm boy extremely agitated. "I was really afraid. I thought he was going to have a fit, or a seizure or something," she says. They drove out of the cemetery grounds as quickly as possible. That is the only time Carol has seen her son have such a difficult reaction with reference to his psychic ability. Most often he takes things in amazing stride.

The child has also simply "known" things, such as when car accidents were on the horizon, just as his mother has. "One time he said, 'Don't go down that road (in Hamilton/Mason),'" recalls Carol. "'There's been an accident and there are two dead people.'" Tragically, they found out later that there had been a crash and that two cheerleaders had lost their lives.

Right before the tornadoes hit and decimated that Kansas town in 2007, Carol's son had told his mom that there would be a lot of places in Kansas where the lights would be out and the homes would be gone. The next day there was that massive tornado in Kansas. That's a lot for a little boy to digest.

Angry soldiers at Arlington Cemetery. *Courtesy of Sean McHugh*

Also on a grand scale, Carol's daughter, who is younger than her son, sensed the Minneapolis bridge collapse a week before it happened. "She started freaking out every time we went over bridges and saying, 'Mom, don't you understand? Other people are gonna die; they're not gonna be around. They're gonna get stuck under the bridge!'" Sadly that bridge collapse was a tragedy of epic proportions.

"Okay, I've got two," Carol recalls thinking, once she realized her daughter had "felt" the bridge collapse coming. In order to save her children from being singled out by other children or adults she's talked to them about what they tell their friends and others outside the family.

"We don't make it a big deal," says Carol. "There's things we talk about and things we don't," she told them. The things they see happening before they happen fall into the "don't" category.

Carol has made it a point to adapt to these rules as well. "When I get very busy, very stressed, I tend to not get those emotions and when it does come, it pops into my head. "In business, I've decided I'm not gonna say it. I've had people look at me wide-eyed wondering how I knew that," she says. If she gets a warning feeling she will say something to her husband, brother, or friend, for example, but not to business associates anymore.

"With dreams there is a feeling I get and when I wake up, I just know it was one of those dreams," she says. "Now it's come to the point where I just know when it's a thought (whether it's legitimate or a psychic thought) or a random thought like we all have. The hair on my arms might rise up. It's the way it pops in my head. I guess it just comes in a different way. I'm just now in tune to that there's a different way it pops into my brain," Carol says. Or sometimes a feeling in her gut will validate the fleeting emotion/vision.

"There are periods where I am really on or really off," she says. "If I'm on, it can happen (and be correctly validated) five times a day."

"It doesn't come when I want it to," she says with a giggle of exasperation. "Why does this not work (for this or that…)?" Before her father passed away she says she did notice she had an uneasiness/worry about him for the six months leading up to his death, but nothing came with distinct clarity.

"My mother knows big things," she says. "Three days before 911, she felt nauseous. She can usually feel real big negative things," she says. Usually her mom "feels" manmade, human-caused events, but she is unable to hone in on where/what will happen.

In addition to sensing what is on the horizon, her grandmother and mother have each had connection and conversations with people that have passed away. It is true mediumship in the family sense of the word. Her son, too, has this ability as he has seen her father after his demise. He told his mother that he'd seen a man checking out their patio. "That's the first thing my dad would have done," says Carol with a laugh. Her son also "saw" a vision of a dog that Carol had owned years earlier. He told her that the pooch kept trying to get into the hot tub for some reason. Carol recognized the behavior immediately. That is exactly what her dog used to do (and she'd never told her son that, either).

One morning when her son was two, he told his mother that he had had a visitor (a boy specter named Tommy) the night before in his bedroom. Seems that Tommy told her son that he should jump out the window and play with him in the moonlight. Her son's room was on the second floor and if he had chosen to listen to his paranormal visitor, he could have been severely injured or even killed.

"That is the only thing that ever bothered me," says Carol. You can bet his window is secured and thankfully nothing else as disconcerting has occurred since that time.

She's never sure when she will "see" something, nor when her children will, for that matter. While Carol and her son were going to lunch in the cafeteria at Sinclair Community College, for example, he told her he couldn't (wouldn't) go in the elevator. Why? "Because there are people floating around," he simply replied. Turns out the cafeteria on campus is rumored to be one of the hot spots for ghosts.

While living in Salem, Carol says that numerous odd and much more blatant things occurred, courtesy of the ghost in their home. Ball caps would go missing and then a week later she'd find them all on her bed—completely stacked up. One time she was cleaning her home and her cappuccino maker suddenly went flying down the hall. To appease the male spirit she believed was hanging around, Carol would pour him a shot of whiskey and put it on the mantle and invite him to sit a while and watch TV. That worked pretty much every time.

Once they moved to Ohio, the family believed they'd be leaving any ghostly sort of activity back in Salem. "I think we were there (Liberty Heights) about a year and the neighbors would say they saw blue lights coming from our home at three or four in the morning," says Carol.

Two or three different people approached Carol and told her that they would see blue lights coming out of their windows. "It wasn't the same window because the neighbors had different views of the house," she says.

Carol witnessed the blue phenomenon herself, as well. "I awoke one night and there was a blue mist in my bedroom, she says. "I don't know what it was. It was hovering about two feet from me when I was sleeping."

Instead of being alarmed by these colored lights, Carol views them as a comforting sign. "I see it as someone was there checking on me," she says.

In addition to ghostly lights and premonitions, Carol has had some mildly amusing pranks played upon her by unseen forces while in the Dayton-area home as well. The following scenario she believes was likely courtesy of her dearly departed father.

It was Super Bowl Sunday, and her father, who was a big Patriot's fan "would have wanted me to know he was there," says Carol. "Anyway, I went outside (I had all three dogs, Golden Retrievers, and I was hosing them off). As she was heading back in, she found the door was locked. Initially, she was soundly miffed at her husband, who she figured would think it might be funny to strand her out there with wet dogs in the middle of winter, yet she was surprised at how adamantly he denied doing the deed. He pointed out to his wife that the hallway was covered in mud from the dogs and there were no human footprints. "I actually get locked out about four times a year (and blame him every time)," she said. That final evidence convinced her that perhaps it wasn't her husband, but her father, who had passed on, showing her that he was still around and ready to tease her at a moment's notice.

There are other household oddities that have occurred since her father's death, as well. For example, all of the batteries in their smoke alarms exploded at the same time. She called an electrician who replaced all of their smoke alarms...only to have them all explode at the same time again. "I don't know what to tell you," the electrician said. "I've never seen this happen before!"

After her father died, her car battery died; so did her sister's car battery and her aunt's car battery. All of them gave out on the same day. "I said, 'Dad, I love you, I'm glad that you're here, but get out of my car,'" she recalls with a chuckle.

Carol has also noticed that when her kids become ill, their rooms become frigid no matter what the season might be. "I think it's some-body being there to check on them," she says. When her son was young, he had a problem surgery and she said his room was cold for three days. Once her child was better, the room warmed up.

The whole family hears footsteps at night, fairly regularly, and her husband dutifully checks them out, but never encounters a burglar (of the human variety, at least), so he reluctantly admits that things are going on in his household that he just cannot explain. Voices are sometimes heard in the house, although they are indiscernible and you might hear a door open/close as well, she says. Her son still sees the dog that passed away quite a bit, she says. He says the dog often "takes up" a big part of his bed.

The Ohio family seems to encounter oddities wherever they might go. It comes with the psychic territory. While vacationing at a house at Lake Juanita in New York, they experienced doors locking and Carol kept hearing somebody with a childlike voice whisper, "Mommy," and then she'd feel a tug on her clothing.

"It happened the whole time I was at the house. It was pretty distressing," she says. "Why me?" She says she wondered, worry-ing about the poor ghostly child. "Can't I just go on vacation for a week?

"I do want to say—other than one instance where my son was told to jump out of his window to play with 'Tommy,' nothing in our house has ever been uncomfortable, and I have always felt that whatever was there, was either there to say, 'hello' or to watch over us. What I find interesting is when others witness the stuff in our house, like the neighbors and the lights. It does sort of validate it for me. But then again, I am pretty comfortable with it, seeing as it has always been around me."

Chapter 15

The Red Room on Sullivan Road

The house on Sullivan Road was a local landmark. According to Dayton Ghost Hunters Society (DGHS) Vice President Mike Kmucha, back when he was growing up in Huber Heights (a suburb of Dayton), every local kid knew about Sullivan Road (and their parents probably did, too). The house was the former abode of one, elusive Mr. Sullivan and most anybody you asked would agree that it was haunted, says Kmucha. The fact that it became abandoned and likely haunted made it the place to go for fun-loving teens—whether they were looking for a scare, a chance to connect with the opposite sex or both.

Lovers Lane

"We were all young guys looking out to get one thing," admits Kmucha, "and anytime during the summertime the big thing to do was find some girls and take them down this street by the house."

Although the teen boys were concentrating on the young ladies for the majority of their duration at the site, the fact that something truly was odd about this house (and the land) was never fully out of their adolescent minds.

"On the street in front of the house, it was foggy," recalls Kmucha. "It was always foggy in front of that house—but only in summertime." Wintertime was sans fog; fall and spring were fog-less, too. What could have caused such a thick fog in perpetuity all summer long?

"I mean, I'm sure (somehow) that's explainable...um, maybe," he laughs. Still, this wasn't light fog, either. This was the kind of fog worthy of a John Carpenter flick.

"You had to go like five mph because of how thick it was," he says. The entire road was not foggy, either; just the section around Mr. Sullivan's old house and property. "The whole outer barrier of his property was always foggy," he shares.

Given the oddity of the fog, the rumors behind the house, and the fact that they had nothing better to do, one afternoon Kmucha's crowd decided to take the plunge and delve past the exterior of the property and venture inside the house on Sullivan Road. It was the summer of 1987.

The House

"We decided we were gonna be brave and on a Saturday afternoon, go investigate Sullivan's house. You know, young boys, we think we're invincible, blah, blah, blah," recalls Kmucha, "so we go inside the house."

What greeted them were the walls of an abandoned structure that had at one time been somebody's grand home.

"There was no furniture in the place," he says. The friends wandered off in separate directions. "I went upstairs, and, of course, when you go up old wooden floors," notes Kmucha, "they creak and everything."

All of the bedrooms in the house were on the second floor, he recalls, and judging by the floor plan, this house was once a mighty fine place to call home.

"The bedrooms all had the old fireplaces with the mantels and everything," he says. Truly impressive and grand. What really floored him about the house was found further down the hall, however.

"When I went to the very back room on the north side of the house, I came to a bedroom that had red carpet," he shares. But that wasn't all.

"The room also had red walls and a red ceiling," recalls Kmucha. "I'm talking fire-engine red." It took this then-teenaged boy a moment to absorb such a bold-colored sight. After all, not many people have walked into a room that was bathed all in red. While soaking all the crimson in, Kmucha eventually noticed something else across the room.

"I saw a cup, like a little plastic see-through cup with a rose sticking in it," he says. "It was sitting on the mantle over the old fireplace." (Dare we inquire as to the color of this lovely flower?)

"You guessed it," says Kmucha. "Yep, the rose was red." Assuming that the petaled wonder was plastic or silk, yet intrigued beyond measure, he propelled forward across the dusty carpeted floor. "The fireplace was in the back of the room," explains Kmucha. "You'd have to walk all the way through the room to get to it."

"Well, I walk through the room," he recounts, "and I (get right up to the mantel) and I realize that the rose is real. It is sitting in two, two-and-a-half, inches of water on the mantel. When I turned around to tell my buddies, 'Man, this rose is real, we need to go!' you could see my footprints in the years of dust that had built up on the carpet."

Those footprints were not what startled Kmucha, however. What gave him pause was the fact that there were no other footprints to be found. How had that real red rose and cup of water made it across the room and onto the mantel without so much as an inkling of a dusty trail?

"I had the only footprints in the whole room," says Kmucha. "How did that rose get there? If it had been put there years before it would have been long dead and the water would have evaporated." Multiple scenarios raced through his mind. Come on! Get real! Did the rose fly over there by itself?

He will never know how that rose got there, and neither will we. The house has since been torn down by the city with very little remnants remaining. The legend of the Sullivan House is not ripe in the minds of the new generation; but it still lingers in the thoughts and memories of those boys from Huber Heights who went there for a thrill; and courtesy of an unknown, romantic visitor to that red room, they sure got one.

Chapter 16

The Amber Rose

The Amber Rose Restaurant is a staple of Dayton, and has been for close to a century. Even though it did not begin as a restaurant, the structure has been an important part of the area's history. It was erected by a Polish immigrant and initially served as the area's general store. In addition to selling necessary goods, it was the place to meet, greet, and catch up for the Polish community for many years.

The Amber Rose at Twilight.

The building was lovingly restored in 1990 (listed on the National Register of Historic Places in 1992) and resurrected as a top-notch dining establishment, featuring a variety of cuisines including Eastern European and German. It's a bustling place with a jovial over-all feel. Joe Castellano is the proud owner of the fine (and wonderfully haunted) establishment.

According to Shelly Rosenkrantz, the resident jack-of-all-trades at the Amber Rose, the building was not only the General Store but also came complete with a one-lane bowling alley in the basement. Several generations lived there on site, and Rosenkrantz said she was told that, at one time, there were nine staircases in the house.

According to manager Emily Bardonero, the owners of the store would live upstairs. Chickie is the female ghost that is most widely believed to haunt the site and she is often detected upstairs in the former living quarters. "I think Chickie was a nickname she had as a kid," says Rosenkrantz. "She died a spinster," she adds.

Getting the Literal Cold Shoulder

According to those in the know, Chickie enjoys messing with employees, patrons, and visiting workers alike. For example, two of their mechanics were upstairs trying to fix the air conditioner one day, and one of the fellows suddenly felt the unmistakable sensation of two frigid hands in a vise-grip upon his shoulders. An icy, paranormal touch. He was not amused.

"I'm never coming back," he told the Amber Rose staff. "From now on, call somebody else."

Although the entire building seems to be fair game for a visit from this spinster from the past, it is the lowest level of the structure that seems to evoke the most intense issues with wait staff. Turns out, there might be somebody else on the specter scale hovering around down there, however.

"Nobody likes to go downstairs," says Rosenkrantz. The vibe is far more uncomfortable in the bowels of the building and being down there alone, especially, is too much for some of the employees. Is it Chickie that is down there, however? Perhaps not.

"I think there's somebody, a male presence, in the basement," Rosenkrantz says. This might help explain the uneasiness the employees have in its midst. "Somebody next door saw a male in the basement after hours," Rosenkrantz expounds. "She called the restaurant and told the cleaning man and when he investigated, he found no one. (The caller) said the man she saw was wearing a hat and a long coat (like a cowboy would wear)." This would help explain why the vibe is so different in the basement than it is within the rest of the structure.

One waitress was down alone in the basement and saw her shadow on the wall; big deal, right?   Yes, it was, because she also saw another shadow as well, and she was the only one downstairs. The shadow was that of a man. "I started believing then," the waitress shares. They believe that the fellow (ghost) downstairs might be named Robert. They just found out about Robert last year. According to a visiting psychic, Robert was employed on the site in the 1920s or 1930s. The psychic also said she saw him with an apron on. Robert seems to stay put in the basement, but Chickie seems to get around the rest of the place.

Chickie has her own unique ways of making herself known at any time of day or night. During a bustling evening, stunned bartenders have seen glasses shoot right off the shelf. They don't just tip over and drop either. "They have been thrown clear across the walkway and shattered on the bar top. "It happens a lot," says Bardonaro.

It is not only the dedicated employees that have witnessed this strange phenomena, either. According to those in the know, customers have said that their silverware moves, and that their lemon wedges "jump" off of their ice tea glasses. The fellow who works as the deli guru was chatting up the waitress while making a sandwich last year and his can of no-stick spray raised up and levitated, and then slammed down. The waitress said, "Did you see that?" Ah, yep, he sure did.

Bardonaro has worked at the Amber Rose Restaurant for over ten years and she is quite familiar with Chickie's antics. "TVs have turned on and off often." Bardonaro also recalls an incident with flying objects. "The back room downstairs in the pantry has very large shelves and two very large vessels filled with dressings that flew off of the shelf."

Despite such blatant paranormal antics, Bardonaro has quite a fondness for the establishment and for Chickie. "I met my husband here. He was manager at that time, and I was waitressing," she notes. Her husband had his own strange encounters on-site. The most incredible of which, occurred in the upstairs.

"There is a center room in the upstairs portion of the structure that has doors on either side. One of the sides faces a hall with a window," she notes. One evening, Bardonaro's husband-to-be was strolling past this section and witnessed a blue flash in that room. He assumed it was a bolt of lightning, she says, until he realized that the door to the other side (the one facing the window was shut). Upon further investigation, he believes that the blue flash seemed

Members of the Dayton Ghost Hunters Society meet at the Amber Rose for a "Scare and Share." "Chickie," a spinster spirit, is said to haunt the site.

to emanate from the attic (which has a pull down stairwell in that middle room).

In addition to her electric output, Chickie enjoys flinging things around, and does so quite often. "Dishes will fall—lots of them," says Bardonaro. "The staff will leave the room, come back, and find them on the floor."

Although she is an active ghost on the whole, months will go by and nothing will happen. A lot of times change can cause things to flare up, says Bardonaro. "We don't have a lot of turnover in staff, but when we do, the change gets Chickie going. When somebody new starts, things start happening."

Bardonaro and Rosenkrantz recall the time a group of people who had reserved the room upstairs for a party asked if anything ever happened courtesy of the ghost up there. The waitress assured them that, indeed, paranormal things did happen up there, yet "they didn't believe me," she says.

It was right about that time that a bottle of wine flew off of the rolling bar and landed four or five feet away, Rosenkrantz says. No person (no living person) was near that area at the time. She grins and recounted what she heard the customers screech out at that moment: "'Oh my God!'"

Rosenkrantz's delighted response was quick and to the point. "'See? She's here! I told ya!'"

Rosenkrantz does what needs doing at the Amber Rose; she is bartender, server, and caterer and those roles put her in multiple scenarios throughout the building. She recalls when a newer employee told her that she saw somebody in the hallway and then heard them go in the bathroom. The newbie thought it was the bartender in there, as she heard him washing his hands. She was yapping away, talking to him and she heard the paper towel holder working. Exasperated, at his lack of response, she finally called out to him, "'Why aren't you answering me?'" What a shock for this waitress to see the bartender come trudging up the basement stairs; and when she checked there was nobody in the bathroom at all.

In addition to giving some men the cold shoulder, Chickie loves messing with the dish machine and the ice machine in the downstairs kitchen. They are about ten feet apart and every once in a while the scoop from the ice machine will zip across the dishes, landing in the dish tank. She also enjoys fooling around with the credit card machines. They will all suddenly turn on and start ringing out.

Holidays seem to bring out the imp in the ghosts, as October and Christmas are really active. It is not that uncommon to find all the silverware, which had been set for an upcoming party the night before piled up in middle of the tables. Rosenkrantz indicates that people have seen what they describe as a "hazy ball" in the upstairs corner. She's been known to pause and say, ""Hey, Chickie, how ya doing?'" and go on with her duties.

The Amber Rose: Home of the Brave (Cleaning Man)

One former employee lived right around the restaurant and noticed late at night—about two o'clock in the morning—that the lights were on in the attic. She called and told the cleaning man and he went up there only to discover that there was no light bulb in the fixture. This poor fellow is sent up and down, round and round the restaurant as each odd scenario comes up.

Jennifer Combs, who is a caterer and server at the Amber Rose, has her own true accounts to share. She has seen Chickie herself as have some patrons. When asked if the customers who've seen her have described her as old and spinster-like, Combs said, yes. "She was in her forties…"

The Amber Rose, lunchtime.

Whoa, no wonder Chickie is flinging things around. Many people would find recoil at such a proclamation (including me). Combs quickly rebounds to say she died in her early 50s—much more spinster appropriate. Say, what?

Regardless, Chickie has been hanging around the Amber Rose building for many years and one thing is for certain: Things don't tend to get too boring in the Amber Rose. "It's kind of neat (having Chickie around)," says Rosenkrantz. "A little different, right?" Bardonaro nods affirmatively.

Remember: If you stop by the historic site for some great grub and a drink, hang onto your lemon wedges and make sure to tip your glass to Chickie (before she decides to do it for you!).

The Amber Rose Restaurant is located on 1470 Valley Street in Dayton, Ohio.

Chapter 17

The Doofley House

The Doofley House is a three-floor mansion in the city of Dayton, Montgomery County, Ohio.

Dayton Ghost Hunters Society (DGHS) historian and investigator Penny Massie had an electric account while visiting the site for an investigation. Massie, who has been with the group since July of 2006, has had a fascination with the paranormal/unexplained for much of her life. She has investigated places outside of her Ohio home, including The Stanley Hotel in Colorado. "It's a beautiful hotel with an interesting history," she shares. "I got to meet T.A.P.S. there and investigated with them.

"I've had several experiences in my life," shares Massie, "and so I've had so many questions that I couldn't answer. It used to be quite often when I was younger, but now it varies. Something usually happens when I least expect it. My curiosity brought me to this group, and it has been one of the best things I've ever done with my life. I've really learned a lot about the paranormal since joining, and I've also learned about the value of friendship."

The summer of 2007 in particular was an active one, paranormally speaking, for Massie. In April of that year, Massie found herself on the top floor of The Doofley House. It was an amazing structure, to be sure. "I know it's about 200 years old," she shares, "and there were soldiers there at one time. There used to be a ballroom on the third floor where they held dances."

This place sure is big. According to Massie, the house was built in 1909, and has at least twenty-four rooms. Massie's odd experience occurred while she was traversing the third floor within the magnificent structure. "It happened within the first room on the left," she recalls. "I took my dowsing rods. I had gone up there because the person who was watching the computer monitor was saying he was hearing noises on the third floor. I asked the rods to take me to the spirit. They led down the hall to the first room on the left. Then they took me to the right of the room and then swiveled all the way around to the left of the room. They then stopped on a green rug and the rods crossed. At that moment," Massie shares, "it felt like electricity came up my arms through the rods and began to spread all over my body. The hairs on my arm began to stand up. It was the strangest feeling. But then it got to the point where I couldn't move or respond to someone who was calling my name." It was as if she were possessed. And as if these physical sensations weren't enough, she then began experiencing emotional offshoots.

"I then became very depressed, like I was feeling someone else's feelings. My knees began to get weak, and I can remember one of the guys coming in the door after me. I just seemed to have snapped out of what was happening, but was so weak and shaking, I could barely stand. I did quickly snap a picture before I was taken downstairs to recuperate. After developing my picture, which was on APS film, I had what seemed to be an orb (ball of energy) over the green rug where the rods had crossed. The funny part was that another lady from the group took a picture in the same spot with a digital camera and she got the same looking orb. I was extremely excited (not frightened).

The DGHS group members knew something was going on. "They saw what was happening to me," notes Massie. Since the two members took a photo of the same spot with different types of cameras, and both came away with orbs, it does make the group question if something was hanging around there.

"Even though our group doesn't believe in too many orbs, it's kind of a coincidence that two of us caught the same thing on our cameras," Massie says.

When Massive senses some sort of entity might be in her midst, she often gets chills. "Also, sometimes it feels sort of like electricity running through my body," she adds.

"I don't like to actually say a place is haunted unless you can back up an experience with some kind of physical evidence," notes the historian and investigator. "Pictures are great, and sometimes they may look like something is going on, but there can be another explanation for it. It's really nice to get an EVP (electronic voice phenomenon), or something captured on video, but you also need to be able to rule out other possibilities. If more than one person has an experience and it can be backed up with evidence that's not normal and can't be explained, then I usually call the place haunted."

Connie Holder (DGHS investigator and intuitive) went through the mansion for the walk through but wasn't there for the investigation, which happened days later. In the initial interview, they went up to the top floor and Holder was at the back of the pack and didn't hear any of the stories or the research they had done. Turns out her back was hurting, so she went off into a side room upstairs and gingerly rested upon a settee to aid her aching lumbar region. Slowly, she leaned back.

"When I did, it felt like there was something sharp in my back (like a metal bar)," she says. She looked back and nothing was there, so she tried to lean back again and got the feeling of the metal bar there—only this time coupled with an intense feeling of sadness. Holder pushed on the back of the couch and felt absolutely nothing protruding at all. There was no metal bar. She told DGHS members that they should definitely put a camera in that room when they investigated the place. The group did so and they did catch an anomaly on video, but right after, that the video somehow became erased—to everyone's dismay. This was the precise room where Massie had her experience with the dowsing rods and the photographs by two members of the same area that showed the same orb at the same time.

Why was there such a drenching feeling of sorrow in that upstairs room for not one, but several of the DGHS members? They cannot pinpoint the cause or the potential entity evoking it. Given their initial video and two members' experiences and those similar photographs, they do believe that there is something hovering in that room; whether it's residual or active is unknown as well.

Unfortunately, scenarios such as the film erasing happen all too often in the ghost hunting biz; and seasoned group members have learned to go with the flow and keep plugging away.

Massie, for one, plans on continuing to hunt the elusive entities for a long time. "It's all about finding answers, helping people, making friends, and having fun in the process. It gives you an adrenaline rush, kind of like being on a roller coaster, while also giving hope that there is an afterlife," she shares.

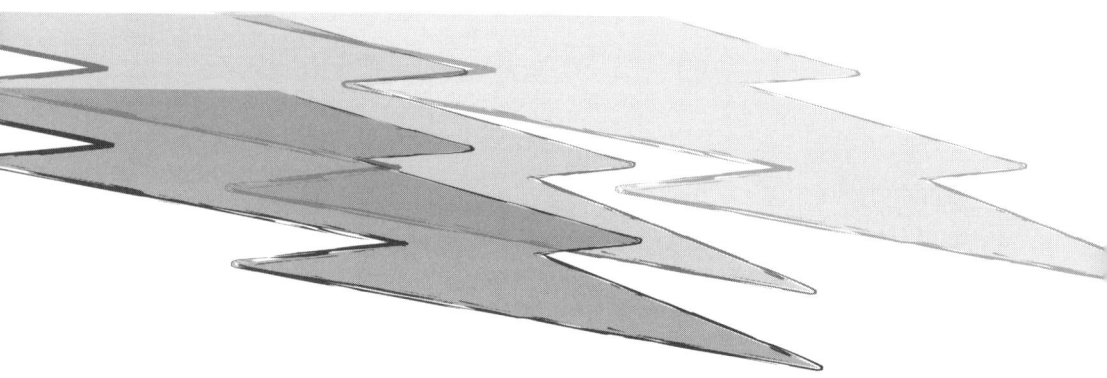

Chapter 18

The Old Courthouse

According to Curt Dalton, author of multiple books and avid local Dayton historian, www.daytonhistorybooks.citymaax.com, the Old Courthouse in Dayton holds much in the way of history and reverberating emotions. Moans and the sounds of chains rattling in the basement, invisible footsteps trod aimlessly down cold halls, a scream erupts from the bowels of a building, one that only matronly despair can elicit. Did you see that misty blob? These are some of the accounts that have been heard and seen throughout the years in the Old Courthouse on 3rd and Main Streets in downtown Dayton.

The (haunted) Old Courthouse in Montgomery County, Ohio.

Today, the place is not just a potentially haunted arena; it is an impressive historical site. Many years before it was the local jailhouse and also served as the final stop for some, it was where the rope draped around necks deemed guilty and bodies were dropped. The old gallows remain today.

The gorgeous Greek Revival Courthouse building is believed to be the best in the country. It was dedicated on April 12, 1850, and was crafted from stone, brick, and limestone. The site was the hub for Montgomery County law enforcement and government for many years.

Before his election, Abraham Lincoln wowed the crowds with his address there in September of 1859. Other presidents who visited the important site include Bill Clinton, Ronald Reagen, Gerald Ford, Lyndon B. Johnson, Andrew Johnson, James Garfield, and John F. Kennedy. Daytonians understood the relevance of this building, and restoration for the Old Courthouse was completed in 2005. Today the community utilizes the site for parties, meetings, events, and receptions. Mammoth pillars mark the entrance atop a grand cascade of cement steps that serve as the perfect place for downtowners to sit and munch their lunch on a sunny spring day. Five massive American flags drape down between the pillars, calling forth patriotism and pride.

This building has lasted through several wars and a severe economic crunch on the town, and remains standing tall.

People worked there, were imprisoned there, visited there, and died there, and now it appears that some who died there still remain. For example, the ghost of John McAfee was widely believed to have been seen many years after his execution took place. McAfee was troubled at a young age. He had a rough childhood and fled his hometown in his early teens. He worked odd jobs from town to town and ultimately met and married a Pennsylvanian when he was nineteen. The couple moved to the Dayton area and had a child. He grew tired of his life and his wife, however, and it wasn't long before McAfee roamed yet again…this time into the bed of the woman who lived right next door.

Opting to rid himself of his marriage and be with his mistress, he tried poisoning his wife in 1824. It didn't quite kill her, so he finished the job by clasping his hands firmly around her young neck until she finally breathed no more.

McAfee was eventually found out and doomed to an end by the same means his wife had met her Maker; only his breathing would be ceased via the noose. The end was not swift and quick, however, as it was written that his body "quivered" for many minutes before succumbing to asphyxia.

Legend has it that in the early years following his execution, McAfee's ghost would tend to hover around the area, especially whenever marchers or musicians were on Third Street in the evening. During such occasions, the misty form of the man would float west down the road. Numerous individuals witnessed this.

In addition, the *Dayton Daily Journal* reported a sighting of McAfee's apparition by a jailhouse employee in 1884. The sheriff at that time found the employee hovering in the boiler room, extremely distressed. The fellow 'fessed up that he had witnessed something in the southwest corner of the old courthouse that freaked him out— enough to make him up and quit his job. He indicated that he had not only seen the apparition of McAfee, he had actually run directly into the "tall, clammy thing," its finger gesturing for the fellow to follow it to the river bridge. (Oddly enough, he declined to do so.) Toss in the incessant rattling of bones and chains, and that was enough to convince the distraught fellow that no amount of wages was worth hanging around the old courthouse ever again. Turns out that the area that the ghost had been gesturing toward was the location of McAfee's hanging many years prior.

Another ghost that appeared in the old courthouse came to the cell of a man named James Murphy. Seems that Murphy was slated for a life of despair from birth. He was born in 1856, and mostly raised by his father (his mother passed away when he was quite little), and his old man was unable to bestow the kind of guidance or devotion upon him that was needed. The result was a teen that ended up in the "Chain Gang," a notorious, vicious group of prowling youth in Dayton. Seems he held the title in the gang of "lieutenant," and found a disgusting sense of fulfillment in being cruel to animals and family members. The curly-haired boy with the long, high forehead and gray eyes was a force in town, a force to be avoided. His actions ebbed to the point where Murphy ultimately murdered a fellow by cramming a knife into the man's torso; all because he had kicked him/his gang out of a private wedding party reception minutes prior. Of course, Murphy was drinking at the time the incident occurred.

Public outrage followed and Murphy was jailed and put on trial. The outcome was a hung jury, which outraged the locals all the more. A second trial was scheduled. It was while awaiting that trial on one dank spring night that an otherworldly female sound screeched throughout the jailhouse walls. The ear-splitting wail tore a hole through the night's silence. It roused sleepers and goose bumps,

and sped up heartbeats of the prisoners and the jail staff alike. A search of the all-male premises was immediately undertaken, but no female was found.

Later it was revealed by Murphy that he had not only heard the God-awful wailing, he'd actually seen the woman from whom the scream hailed. It was the ghost of the woman who had given birth to him some twenty years prior—Murphy's very own mother. The specter was in complete and utter despair from beyond the grave, and the murderous youth knew the second that he saw her that his fate was sealed; he would most certainly die by the noose. He was right. Little did he know, however, that his death by noose wouldn't be a slam dunk.

Following this visit from beyond, Murphy had confessed his sins to the local priest and come to express sorrow and remorse for his actions. He had seemed to find a semblance of peace, which was good because he certainly was going to need it. Gallows don't erect themselves and Murphy was privy to the creation of the death-inducing structure since it was built within sight of the convicted man's cell. Murphy also watched the men as they tested the durability of the long hemp via a dangling bucket filled with nails (this was done to be sure the rope would hold).

However, nothing was ever sure in Murphy's life, nor would it be in his death. The day of his execution arrived and Murphy was led to the rope, the black hood then draped over his head. He was calm, ready. Soon the trapdoor beneath his boots opened. Instead of working as it was supposed to, however, the rope tugged a moment then snapped. Murphy plummeted to the floor and was knocked unconscious; but only for a moment. Horrifically the addled young man woke up in time to grasp the reality of what had happened, and the undeniable heartache and shock of what he would once again have to face. The reporters who were there to record the hanging documented that this young man's features were constricted in sheer terror. It was a relief for all those in attendance when the second rope was secured to the gallows and the hood was again placed upon his trembling head to block their view. This time, however, before the floor gave way, Murphy's fingers reached out and grabbed onto the deputy; clutching him with such urgency and fear that it seemed as if he would never release his grip. It took the quick-thinking, consoling words of the priest to cajole Murphy into letting loose of the deputy's garment and allow his ultimate journey to commence. The floor opened. The body dropped. This time, to the relief of all, the rope held. A full seventeen minutes later, Murphy exhaled his last breath. What a way to go.

No matter what people might have thought of this boy, barely turned man, or his violent actions, most agreed that it was a very sad life and an excruciating way to die. His mother's death meant she'd been unable to raise her child, yet she was still tortured by watching him ruin his life from beyond; talk about excruciating circumstances.

Is Murphy still around that place? Is his mother? No one knows for sure. McAfee probably knows, but so far, he ain't talking.

The Old Courthouse is located in downtown Dayton on Third and Main Streets.

Chapter 19

The Elberfeld Place

Vella Elberfeld and her daughter, Cindy Shaffer, didn't go looking for ghosts in their house—quite the opposite. They just sort of made themselves known to the entire family. The Elberfeld family consisted of the parents, their four children (three boys and Shaffer), and three foster children (all girls). Turns out everybody in this large clan knew something or someone else was hanging around their home in Springfield, Ohio.

They lived in the house for many years and had many odd things occur over that time. The foster children, however, were especially displeased with the other household occupants and they often admitted that they were afraid.

There was one particular foster girl who had the most profound thing occur with the ghost ("Miss No Nonsense" as Shaffer refers to her) as she was getting ready to go into the Army.

"She had been told that she needed to lose some weight beforehand." Shaffer said she went through this whole ordeal to lose the pounds, including wearing the trash bags while working out. "One time she was alone in the house and she was exercising, and she said she felt like somebody slapped her on the butt; hard," says Shaffer. "She then heard a voice and what was said to her was something no one else in the whole world could have ever known about. She was never so glad to get the hell out of the house," she adds.

It wasn't just the human family members who noticed something strange was going on, says Shaffer. Snert, the little family toy poodle would periodically yelp out of the blue and run behind the chair... they had no idea what caused their pooch to suddenly screech and scamper, but the foster girls likely had their own suspicions.

"The house always creaked and made noises; it sounded like people walking, but we just chalked it up to the age of the house," says Elberfeld, adding that the kids were afraid to go into the attic and the basement, but Elberfeld wasn't. "I was probably in the fifth grade when we moved there," says Shaffer. "One day, the man we bought the house from came over. My brother and I were raking leaves in the front yard and he had just moved down the street. He pulled up and laughed and said, 'You know the house is haunted, right?' He then added that it was his own son who haunted the house. We kind of blew it off but we always noticed after that that if he came over to visit Dad there was more (paranormal) stuff going on after that. His son was supposedly shot down in WWII and his body was never recovered."

Lots of odd things would take place during those first few years. "Doors would open by themselves, you'd hear steps when there wasn't anybody upstairs," recalls Shaffer. "Yeah, windows and doors seemed to open a lot by themselves. Odd things like that, but it never scared us too much; it was more almost like, 'Okay...'"

"My friends knew (the house was haunted)," says Shaffer. "Everybody just kind of ended up taking it for granted after a while. According to the Dayton woman, there were two different ghosts on site. One of them seemed to have more of a female presence while the other came across as a male presence.

Cindy Shaffer's girls pose in front of the Elberfeld House in Springfield, Ohio. (It has since been torn down)

Shaffer believed that the male ghost was more of a prankster and did things as a joke and/or to scare you, while the female entity was the kinder one. One evening, when only Elberfeld and her husband and son were home, they witnessed something strange. Her son was downstairs watching TV and Elberfeld asked him if he planned on being up for a while, as she was going to bed. He said, yes, he would be up, so Elberfeld asked her son to turn out the lights before he came upstairs. "I went up," says Elberfeld, "and we had the hall light out, and I had just gone into the bedroom and (we) saw something (white) go by the bedroom door. My husband says, "'Who was that?'" recalls Elberfeld. "I said, 'I don't know. Chuck is still downstairs. I just left him down there watching television.'"

Elberfeld went down the hall toward her son's bedroom to see if he was in there. She did this even though she knew that he couldn't have gone up the stairs that fast. "I got to the bedroom door, and I didn't see anything," Elberfeld notes, adding, "I was afraid to go in. So I told my husband that I was going to go back downstairs and see if Chuck was there."

"I went down the steps," recalls Elberfeld, "and Chuck said 'What ya doing?' I told him I was going to take some of my pills. I didn't want to scare him," she adds. "I just wanted to see if anybody was down there. I didn't see anything and went out and messed around in the medicine cabinet for a few minutes, and got a glass of water." She trudged back up the steps.

Chuck then called out to his mom, "What are you doing now?" She replied that she was going back to bed. "But I already saw you go upstairs," he'd said.

Chuck confessed later to his mother that he had also seen somebody go through the living room and down into the basement that same night after Elberfeld had gone upstairs. Someone (something?) was certainly making the rounds that night, that's for sure.

"I went back upstairs and told my husband that there's nobody down there but Chuck," says Elberfeld, "and I didn't see anybody in the room."

"Well I saw somebody," her husband replied, knowing full well his wife had also.

"Of course it was a rather sleepless night," says Elberfeld with a chuckle. Another time her husband had already retired for the night and Elberfeld was doing her usual routine of locking up the house. "We used the side door more than we did the front and back door," says Elberfeld, "and I started to lock the basement door because I was always afraid somebody would come through the side door and go down to the basement and be down there. So anyhow, I tried to hold the door shut and started to turn the key." What happened next sent the woman's heart racing.

"The doorknob started twisting," she says. "I grabbed hold of the door knob and put my foot against the door but I just couldn't hold the doorknob still. I wasn't strong enough to be able to hold it. It would just twitter, twitter, twitter back and forth. If there was a spring in there that did that, it surely couldn't be strong enough to hold it!" "I yelled for my husband," she recalls. "I said, 'Come down here! Somebody's in the basement!'"

Elberfeld's husband came fast. "Down he comes running with his gun in his hands," says Elberfeld, "and I didn't even know he had one within reach! I was scared to death."

Shaffer also came running and was in the kitchen when the basement door knob turned repeatedly by itself. "The door knob was moving in my mom's hand and she could not hold it still," she says. "I saw that, everybody saw that."

Panicked, Elberfeld turned on the basement light and dropped to the floor. "I got down on my knees and I looked under the door," she shares, "and I could just make out that our cat was sitting right on the landing. Don't shoot, the cat's sitting down there!" she told her husband. He didn't fire. Instead, he declared that he was going to go outside and check things out from that angle.

"He walked all around the house, and he didn't see anything," Elberfeld shares. Enough time had lapsed without incident, so by the time he returned, their nerves had settled and curiosity had surfaced. "When he came back in, we went down and all through the basement but we didn't see anything or anybody," she says. "So I don't know what that was that was holding the door knob. It was another sleepless night."

At the time, she admits that she was far more worried and afraid that the intruder was a burglar versus a specter. Despite the fear, whatever or whomever was at that house did not seem like a malevolent presence to Elberfeld.

After those experiences, Shaffer's dad changed his tune about not believing in ghosts; but only with the children. "After he saw the ghost, he took us kids aside and told us that we weren't allowed to tell anybody about it because if he ever wanted to sell the house, nobody would want to buy a haunted house. It's funny because my dad was not the kind of person who ever believed in things like that. He would have never in a million years ever believed, if he hadn't seen it," she shares.

The specter sightings continued on through the generations. "My kids, when they were babies, would be holding their arms up to be picked up and nobody was there," says Shaffer. "They could tell somebody was there, but we couldn't see anyone, and that happened really frequently." This was a bit unnerving for the adults, but they were not worried about the twins' safety or anything. In fact, the kinder ghost sometimes even came through for Shaffer in a pinch. "There were times when I would come home and not have my key and I would be locked out," she recalls. "I would try the door and it was definitely locked. I'd be looking for the key. Did I put it back in the (spot outside) last time? Nope, I didn't, and I would be sitting on the front steps waiting for somebody to come home. All of the sudden, I would hear the sound of the door opening. I would look and the door would be partially open and unlocked. That happened more than once," she says with a laugh. Sometimes Shaffer felt intense gratitude and other times fear, "and sometimes, it was a little of both," she admits. "Sometimes it would bother me a lot," she says. "You get a creeped-out feeling like somebody is watching you, and there were other times that it was kind of almost nice, like you weren't alone. It depended upon who was there (the female ghost or the male)."

Although she came to terms with the ghosts in the house, when she first encountered them it bordered on terrifying. "I used to feel like somebody would be holding me down. Kind of like a heavy weight on me," says Shaffer, "and I would holler for Mom and they would come in and it would go away. That was when we first moved in there. That happened like two or three nights in a row and it scared me really bad.

"There were times that you'd think you saw something and then say, 'Naw,'" recalls Shaffer, "but deep inside you knew you had." Thinking back, Shaffer believes that after the old man who used to live down the street died, the incidences, paranormally speaking, dropped off. The house has since been torn down, but the memories of this large family and their resident entities live on.

Chapter 20

The Hidden Room

"I've been interested in this stuff for years and years and years," says Mike Kmucha. "Even in high school, if they were to say, 'Hey, don't go over there, it's scary!' that's where I'd be" (A nifty example of this can be found in The Red Room chapter of this book).

Since Kmucha, who is the current Vice President of the Dayton Ghost Hunters Society (DGHS), has been partnered with the ghost investigative group, however, he's now in a great position to keep his paranormal interests and knowledge going and growing strong. "Now we ask for permission," he says with a chuckle, "and if they say yes, we investigate it."

The seed for Kmucha's intrigue with what goes bump in the night (and daylight) was planted well before his high school years. "I'm one of those Air Force brats," he says. "We had this place out in Southern California, and I would keep telling my dad that somebody was knocking on the walls of my bedroom. His father told him it was nothing and not to be concerned. This knock, knock, knocking, happened over and over and over, however. So much so, that Kmucha again went to his father, asking for at least some sort of explanation for the strange, rapping sounds. "Naw, it's not anything," his father again insisted but the son persisted. "Finally, my dad said, 'It's probably the birds, running into the wall or the window.'"

Fairly satisfied with this, Kmucha waited for a recurrence so he could verify his father's hypothesis. One summertime night, he got his wish, and when Kmucha heard the pounding yet again, he quickly stuck his head outside the window to see what type of aviary species was causing the commotion. He saw nothing. No birds, no creature at all, yet he still heard all this knocking on the walls. The knocking continued as long as they lived there. The lack of resolution as to the source of the knocking was the impetus for a lifelong love of paranormal investigating. "It more or less started there," says Kmucha, "and I've been weird ever since, I guess," he quips. Kmucha has visited a plethora of potentially haunted places in his duties with DGHS and one of his more memorable investigations occurred recently at a farmhouse in Xenia.

Kmucha says the woman who lived there told his group that she often would hear children's voices, and it sounded like they were playing, laughing, and bouncing a ball. The resident would usually hear these things on the floors above her head. This had been going on for quite a while. What propelled the homeowner to finally contact DGHS was a simple tape recorder. The home owner's sister had asked her if she could borrow her tape recorder for one reason or another. She knew she'd stored it in one of the boxes on the second floor. Phone in hand, the owner of the house went upstairs to locate it. She found the recording device rather quickly and inadvertently hit the record button upon retrieving it. Seems that while she was still chatting with her sister on the phone, the conversation had been recorded. Noticing this, she rewound it and hit play.

Kmucha and the DGHS crew were privy to the result. "She played the tape back and on the tape you hear her talking," he says, "but you also hear something else. "You hear some little kids giggling," recalls Kmucha, "and then you hear a big slam like somebody dropped something real heavy on the wooden floor."

Strangest part was there were no kids on the property and the homeowner hadn't heard any of that giggling or slamming while she was up there chatting with her sibling on the phone. When asked for specifics, Kmucha expounds. "It sounded like a little girl laughing." Whew! No wonder that tape recorder was the impetus for the DGHS investigation there.

"This farmhouse was huge," he notes, and the residents had blocked the upstairs off to save money on heating and cooling. Despite this fact, or perhaps because of it, this restricted area of the house looked to be the paranormal active zone. "So, we got up there," he recalls, "and one of the closets in the house (circa 1920s) had a door in the back of it. The door was a little bit higher than me—I'm six foot tall. I asked the owners, 'What is this for?' and they didn't know," says Kmucha. "I asked if I could open it and they said okay."

Kmucha got down on his knees and was pushing on the door, which was sticking with age (the owner of the house was with him). Finally, the door gave way. "As soon as I opened the door, I had a…uh…" he hesitates. "Well… it was like something went right through me," he notes. "The owner of the house was standing right behind me and when I opened that door a cool breeze went directly through me and knocked her down. All the hair on my arms and the back of my neck stood straight up. I turned around to see her there on the ground." Both the homeowner and investigator were completely taken aback. "She didn't say anything," says Kmucha. Not one word. "She got up and ran downstairs."

Despite the incredible "greeting" the two received, the space beyond the door was not extraordinary by any means. "It was a 10- x 20-foot room," says Kmucha. "It was empty. That was it."

What the heck was it there for? What would have been its purpose? "Back in the older days they used to have a solitary confinement-type of room to put the kid in if they were bad," says Kmucha, "and this room reminded me of that." He admits he's not positive that is the answer, it's just a hypothesis. If correct, Kmucha believes that the energy from such a negative place might have built up over the years; until it was finally released, onto him and the homeowner in one big whoosh!

"Our investigation didn't find any deaths," he shares. "I know it was a working farm and they did used to slaughter animals like cows out back," he says, "but we didn't find anything (evidence-wise) outside, it was just in that closet room."

Just who was that little girl on the tape; and what was behind that force in that secret room are still mysteries, but the validation of the presence of these childlike ghosts might provide the farmhouse resident in Xenia, Ohio, with the knowledge that it really wasn't just her imagination—therefore, giving her some semblance of peace.

Meanwhile, Kmucha continues his journey with DGHS; exploring the paranormal side of life and death; and enjoying every minute of it.

Chapter 21

Intuitive Janie Kelly and The Pines Tavern

The Pines Tavern in Medway (a tiny, sleepy town that lies just north of Dayton) had many lives before its sudden flame-ridden demise in January of 2001. It was initially built in 1868 as the local elementary schoolhouse. It also was a restaurant and bar and even raised eyebrows as the town brothel.

A variety of people have had a wide assortment of unique experiences at The Pines; Janie Kelly is one of them. It was her mother who owned The Pines for years. According to Kelly, several of her mom's employees had odd things happen while on the job, as well.

For example, there was a bartender who worked part-time and Kelly recalls something that occurred while he was alone and closing up one night. "We all have the (line up chair) routine when closing up at nighttime," shares Kelly. This particular night, the bartender lined the chairs up at the bar nice and neat, just like always, and went into the kitchen to retrieve something. When he returned to the bar area, "he saw that all of the chairs had spun around into the opposite direction," notes Kelly. "He said he couldn't get out of there fast enough," she adds with a chuckle.

"It just happened that one time," says Kelly. "But there were things that happened when I was there." Sadly, her mother, who owned/operated The Pines had a double massive stroke, and Kelly, who was living in Florida at the time, moved back to Ohio to take care of her.

During this time, Kelly was helping to keep the tavern running and lived upstairs. One instance occurred when she was on the phone with her friend, John, as she went downstairs to the bar to get her coffee from the coffee maker. (This was a necessity since the machine upstairs in the apartment was broken).

Kelly was pouring a cup of java this certain morning (as was the routine), when she heard a strange sound emanating from the men's room (which was not routine). "That's odd," she whispered into the phone. "It sounds like there's somebody in the men's room." Kelly's friend asked her if he wanted her to hang up and come over.

"No!" she responded. She didn't want him to hang up; because if somebody was in there and something were to happen to her, she'd want him to know about it. Phone in hand, she tiptoed over to the men's room.

"As I'm opening the door to go inside," says Kelly, "I heard the toilet flush." So did her friend on the phone. Whoa… Kelly was frightened but able to croak out: "Hello? Hello?" to which there came no reply. Unwilling to let it go at that, Kelly crept further into the bathroom where the single stall door was shut. She summoned up her nerves and peered underneath the door.

"I look under the stall and there's no feet!" Kelly says. She pushed opened the stall door in time to see the last of the water swirling in the toilet bowl. She was out of that bathroom quick. She told her friend: "I think I've enough of being down here right now I think I'll finish my coffee upstairs."

Kelly also recalls a particular Saturday when the bar maid hadn't come in that day so she had to open up for the day shift. She notes that there were the usual patrons on site, but there was also another fellow whom Kelly hadn't seen before.

She was busy working behind the bar, which faced out toward the parking lot, while the patrons sitting at the bar had their backs to the lot.

"I saw some guy kind of walking around out there like he was really curious about some of the cars," recalls Kelly. "He was walking with his hands behind his back and he was looking at the cars." This fellow was highly visible, yet not completely normal looking.

"It didn't really look real," she says, "but it was fairly solid where it could have almost been real, and I just didn't say anything because I just wasn't sure. And then someone came in the bar wearing what looked like a pair of pants and a t-shirt and walked right past us toward the ladies room. Then they were just gone.

"I don't believe this!" Kelly recalls saying. "That guy just went into the ladies room." Of course, everybody's back was turned, so they didn't see anything," shares Kelly. "I walked over there and looked in the ladies room and there was nobody in there. I looked around and one guy said, 'I didn't see anybody come in…and this other guy said, 'I saw it; I saw somebody come in.'"

"Well, where did he go?'" Kelly had asked him. The fellow reluctantly replied, "It was just like you said (a man walked into the bar toward the ladies room and disappeared)."

"He didn't seem real disturbed," recalls Kelly. The customer simply shared that he had also seen a fellow walk into the bar and disappear through a wall into the ladies room. He made it clear that he didn't care to discuss it any further than that. Ghosts don't only come out at night," says Kelly. "This was in broad daylight, a Saturday afternoon."

Hairy, Scary Alice

Kelly's brother had his own odd experiences while living there with his mother. He had told her he would see things periodically, but nothing terrifying. More like peculiar-type things.

Kelly recalls when her mother told her she had been awoken one night by a strange woman who grabbed her arm. She saw a hairy-armed woman who looked very stern (and who people have since believed might be a woman named Alice who ran the place in the 1940s and 1950s). "It's been said that Alice had hands just like a man," shares Kelly.

Her mother had plenty of time to witness unexplainable things; she operated the tavern for about eighteen years, but only two episodes were worthy of telling her daughter about. The aforementioned big-handed broad had another meeting with a female specter who came in the night and slapped her mother in the face. Talk about a rude awakening! Her mother somehow found it within herself to mention this to a few, select people and continue on living there and running her business. Brave woman. The Pines burned down in 2001, and Kelly went on with her life; and her paranormal occurrences.

It should be noted that Kelly is one of those people who witnesses the other side more than the average person. "I've seen things before and heard things. I don't do readings, I'm not one of those; but my friends tell me that I should."

Daymares

"I grew up in the Medway area," says Kelly. "And as a small child I had dreams and visions." These would be highly accurate and sometimes intensely traumatic. She was about four years old, for example, when she saw a vision of her cousin getting killed. In her mind, she was a terrified witness as the young boy was run over by his school bus. The moment that the bus hit him, she saw the entire bus turn blood red. "It scared me to death," Kelly recalls.

"I ran down the stairs and tried to tell my mom that I was having this daymare (what she would call her visions)." Her mother didn't understand. Kelly tried as best as her four-year-old vocabulary would allow her to explain the horror of what she'd just seen, but her mother was unable to clearly grasp it.

Not long after that her mother received a frantic call from his sister; she was screaming and in a panic. Seems her son had boarded the bus that morning, then forgotten something in the house. The child ran back inside to get it. The bus driver waited and saw him come out but then the bus driver became distracted with something and could no longer see the boy. He thought he was not coming back out, but in reality the youngster had stopped to tie his shoe. The bus driver switched into drive and ran over him.

From that point on, her life was altered forever. "I was terrified all growing up if I had a bad dream," says Kelly. "It will still happen where people will contact me from the other side and we'll have conversations. It doesn't happen all the time. It's in my dreams. One in particular was a very good friend of mine who passed away while living in Florida from an inoperable brain tumor. He passed maybe three months after I saw him." She had always believed that they would somehow end up together, but it was not to be. These prophetic dreams can come once or twice a year or more frequently.

This person came to Kelly in a dream several times, insisting that she contact his ex-wife so she could settle his estate. Kelly hadn't talked to his ex-wife in three years but was "told" to contact her by her visions.

"I did call her," says Kelly, "and it was kind of an awkward situation and I said, 'I have to ask you: Does Larry visit you? Do you dream about him?' She said, 'Well, I have dreams about him all the time, but it's nothing like a visitation.'"

"Well, he asked me to call you," Kelly told her. "Let me ask you this, are you having difficulty with his estate?" (This was about three years after he had passed.)

Kelly learned that nothing had been settled with the estate and she told her that there was a document that she needed to find that would help to settle things. The woman replied that if Kelly learned precisely which document it was and where it was located, to please let her know.

"He visited with me a couple of times after that," says Kelly, and she told him in one of her dreams that she had expected her grandma to come and visit her but she had never had a visitation from her grandma and that it disappointed her.

"The next time he came, he had my grandma with him," says Kelly with a laugh, adding, "Am I blowing your mind or what?" Meanwhile, there are no more sightings at The Pines Tavern as it is since long gone. "It's just a vacant lot now…" says Kelly, but whether she likes it or not, the intuitive's daymares remain.

Chapter 22

The Magma Mansion

The Magma Mansion is a Dayton manor that has gone through a series of lives, so to speak. The estate was initially massive, well-built, and prestigious and passed between several family members. It ultimately ended up with the city and was, for a time, abandoned: a sad, yet magnificent shell of its former glory. It has since, however, been lovingly refurbished and is privately owned.

J.T. Ryder came upon the place while it was abandoned. "That place was...odd," says Ryder. He would know; Ryder was working for an alarm company in the summer of 1997, and he was on third shift at the house.

"I was the only one; nobody else would stay the night," he says with a chuckle. "It's one of the neatest places, architecturally, because it doesn't look massive on the outside, but when you're inside, you get lost because of the layout."

According to Ryder, there was an entire servants' wing, there were secret panels in the wainscot in the den that moved, and there was even a drop-down movie projection screen. All of the windows were leaded glass and crafted in diamond shapes. "It looked odd," Ryder shares, "like they were out on an angle, which was disconcerting when walking through the place because if you looked out the window, it looked like everything was moving. The owner/builder did this because he wanted it to always look like there was something going on. If you went past it on the outside, it would look like there's lights flickering on, but if you're inside, it was really weird," notes Ryder, "especially with a flashlight."

One night, Ryder received an emergency call (on his night off) from the company he worked for. The fellow who had trained Ryder was at the site. "You've got to get out there," a supervisor told Ryder, "This guy is ready to bail!"

Ryder recalls the incident as clear as if it were last week. "This guy was like 6'4", shaved head, tattoos, massive dude," he says. The fellow was scared to the point of shaking. Something had definitely spooked him, but Ryder never got any real specifics as to what.

"I get there and we're walking around the outside of this place and he's like, 'I don't look up at the windows…' he says, 'there's a window where it looks like somebody is looking out at you.'" The house and grounds were completely abandoned, remember, and faces in the windows did not sit well with the burly security guard at all.

The window his fellow guard was referring to did have a creepy feel, admitted Ryder. "That window was located in what used to be the children's room on the third floor.

"That guy wouldn't even go in the house," says Ryder. "He was so creeped out by the place that he sat out in his car." The fellow's security duties would encompass walking around the house periodically, but as Ryder indicated, he refused to set foot inside.

"I was the only guy who would go in there at night," he adds. Not only was Ryder unafraid of this place; he was actually somewhat enamored. "It was a really cool house," he says, but he does admit that it could definitely freak certain people out and he had his own way of dealing with the creepiness of the place.

Caution, Children at Play

"I put up a station down in the main foyer," he recalls, and he remembers numerous odd sounds emanating from the house. "The thing that I always had happen was, all night, it sounded like children running back and forth upstairs," he says. Ryder dutifully went and checked out the footsteps the first few nights he was on duty, but he never saw anything. After that, he would hear the phantom children running and barely raise an eyebrow. "Why worry about it? They weren't coming after me," he says, matter-of-factly.

Another anomaly in the house had the ring of an imprint haunting. "Right around three o'clock just about every single morning, there was a loud metallic sound that shook the house," recalls Ryder. "I always assumed it was the furnace (a water hammer)," he says. "I didn't find out until the last week I was there that there was no utilities in the house besides electric. There was no water, no gas."

Upon gleaning this information, Ryder's curiosity soared. *What the hell am I hearing?* he asked himself. "It sounded like somebody taking a sledge hammer to a soil pipe. It was a loud, deep metallic bang. You felt it through the floors, all the way through, and it was a three-story house." In addition to the childlike footsteps and the perpetual night clanging, there was a portion of the house that elicited a feeling of dread in Ryder unlike any other.

"There was one room in the northeast corner, second floor, of the house that I could not stand going into," he admits. "Weird thing is, it actually had my favorite bathroom in there. The room was red and black. Gorgeous, but I couldn't stand to be in the bedroom." Why couldn't he stomach that certain room? "It was a feeling of fear, of being followed," he expounds. "A panicky feeling; you're constantly turning around and looking, because you felt like somebody was watching or coming up behind you. I didn't get those feelings in the bathroom, but you had to cross the bedroom to get to the bathroom."

Ryder worked about a month and a half in graveyard security for the house and he was so fascinated with the place that he vid-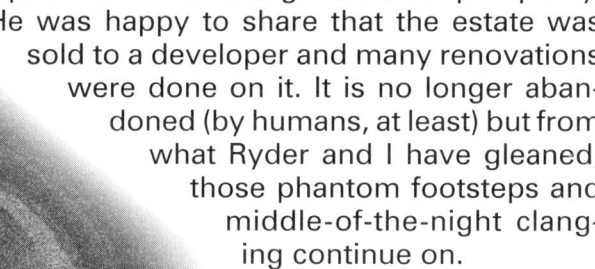eotaped the home and grounds for prosperity. He was happy to share that the estate was sold to a developer and many renovations were done on it. It is no longer abandoned (by humans, at least) but from what Ryder and I have gleaned, those phantom footsteps and middle-of-the-night clanging continue on.

Chapter 23

Library Park

Library Park sets amid the small town center of Miamisburg, Ohio, not far from Dayton. It appears as many a town park might; carpeted in grass, dotted with trees, boasting a gazebo, bandstand, and a billowing water fountain. The difference, however, rests in the underground, haunted history of this park.

Turns out that Library Park was once the Village Cemetery, its origins hailing from around the year 1850. Its purpose was altered dramatically some thirty years after its initiation, due to the sighting of a young woman in white. No, she was not a mourner visiting a dead relative. She was a dead relative.

Library Park in Miamisburg.

This flowing female vision did not just appear once, never to be seen again. Instead, she was a staple in town. As reliable as the postage man and far more intriguing. The woman in white appeared night after night; always at nine o'clock. Most everyone from the town (including high-ranking officials) and those from miles away, learned of her nightly visits and made it a point to be there in the evening to witness this roaming spirit. Despite admitting it was an amazing spectacle, this was not a welcoming sight for this small town outside of Dayton. In fact, it had quite the opposite effect.

The townsfolk became agitated and more and more concerned with the reliable perpetuity of this apparition. So much so, they wanted her gone. They initially attempted to banish her using weaponry. No dice. Since the vision was no longer of flesh and blood, guns, knives and clubs had no effect either physically or emotionally upon the spirit; thus the sightings and panic continued. The next step was to dig up the graves of the Buss family (some believed the vision to be that of the unsettled Buss woman who had been murdered years prior).

The body-moving endeavor did not stop the spooky specter's visits, however, and the frenetic exhumation of body after body continued.

Finally, every single coffin was uprooted and moved to Hill Grove Cemetery up the road. The town then changed what was once the final resting place for so many into the town park.

A newspaper out east, the Frederick, Maryland *Daily News*, wrote an article about the amazing apparition in this small Ohio town. The article, dated March 27, 1884, was entitled: "Real Live Ghost: A Graveyard Apparition that is Scaring a Western Town."

The article read:

"A thousand people surround the graveyard in Miamisburg, a town near Dayton, O., every night to witness the antics of what appears to be a genuine ghost. There is no doubt about the existence of the apparition, as Mayor Marshall, the revenue collector and prominent citizens testify to having seen it. Last night several hundred people, armed with clubs and guns, assaulted the specter, which appeared to be a woman in white. Clubs, bullets and shot tore the air in which the mystic figure floated without disconcerting it in the least. The town turned out en masse today and began exhuming all the bodies in the cemetery. The remains of the Buss family, composed of three people, have already been exhumed. The town is visited daily by hundreds of strangers and none are disappointed as the apparition is always on duty promptly at 9 o'clock. The strange figure was at once recognized by inhabitants of the town as a young lady supposed to have been murdered several years ago. Her attitude while drifting among the graves is one of deep thought, with the head inclined forward and the hands clasped behind."

The sheer numbers of people who had attested to seeing this incredible sight is one for the record books. The media coverage was astounding as well.

The park is warm and inviting today. It does not draw to mind hauntings or exhumation of bodies, that's for sure. The Carnegie Library was erected on-site in the early 1900s, thus followed the gazebo, bandstand, and fountain. The moving of the cemetery does seem to have had the desired effect as the sightings ceased in their regularity, but there have been witnesses that claim to have seen this woman in white as recently as the 1980s, and who knows? Others might have seen a strange white mist at dusk, pacing the grounds where she once was entombed but have not chosen to come forward with the proclamation. Regardless, this woman in white was a vision of the ages; and then some.

Chapter 24

Haunted Lives

Chad Baird moved a lot as a kid. He remembers several houses that were more of a challenge to live in than others. For example, there is a house in Urbana, Ohio, that doesn't hold human occupants well. Baird, who is now a Realtor, lived in that four-bedroom home in Urbana for three or so years, encompassing the time he was in kindergarten and first grade. When they first moved in, around 1976, he recalls that everything seemed normal enough. At least for a family with lots of rambunctious boys. Chad had three brothers, and in addition to the normal trouble that a house full of young men can create, they also experienced the wrath of their parents over something they were not actually guilty of. Somewhat hard to believe, especially for those of us who have parented boys.

Baird chuckles at the memory. "We always got in trouble for taking our toys out and putting them all over the house and down the stairs." The problem was, Baird and his brother's didn't do it. Many kids have the habit of leaving their toys strewn about the house, but not the Baird kids. Although they were by no means perfectly behaved specimens, the one thing they did make sure to do was clean up at nighttime. "We did put our toys away," insists Baird. The kids learned early-on that was one rule that their parents had no leeway with. Yet there were the toys most mornings, splayed around the house. "We had no idea who or what was pulling them out (playing with them?) at night.

"The strict rule was that before, bed we cleaned up the house. We would put our toys away in the toy boxes and in the morning (Mom or Step Dad) would inevitably step upon a mislaid toy," says Baird.

According to this Realtor, no one would ever 'fess up to leaving the toys out, and if nobody 'fessed up, they would all be in trouble. "We'd blame each other," shares Baird, because each boy knew they hadn't done it. So…just who was the real culprit?

Leaving toys strewn in the walkways wasn't the only task that the household ghost would undertake either. "The house had no washer or dryer," explains Baird, "so Mom would lug the laundry about eight houses away to the Laundromat down the street. One time, Mom was at the Laundromat and she got a call from their neighbor," he shares. This neighbor woman used to babysit Baird and his brothers quite often.

'You need to get home!' the neighbor told his mom. 'Your kids are tearing your house apart. Why didn't you just leave them with me?'

Baird's mother was stupefied by this proclamation, since her children were at the Laundromat; in fact, she was watching them play out in the back of the building on the sand pile as she spoke to her neighbor.

"You must be mistaken. My kids are with me," she told her neighbor, who quickly replied, "Well, there's somebody over there and they are tearing your house apart!" His mother scooped up the clothes and her boys and they all raced home where they discovered an extreme mess waiting for them.

"Every one of our toys was strewn around the house," shares Baird. "Everything. And it was not how we had left it." No doubt this made an impression not only on the boys, but their mother, as well.

"Mom believes in ghosts," says Baird. "After that, she started doing research and found out the house was once a prestigious mansion in Urbana. In the day, it was a very nice place."

His mother also discovered that the people that had lived there, a father, mother, and two children, had been in a massive car accident, and everyone in the family had been killed.

Chad Baird, Come on Down!

In addition to the ruckus and toy-leaving antics, other things would happen, too.

"One night Mom had gone out with friends," shares Baird. "My dad was home with us and he was big on ham radios (he had an office set up in the house with his radio equipment). My oldest brother was into it as well." They were all upstairs that night, hanging out in the radio room when Baird left to go downstairs to use the home's only bathroom.

"On my way, I heard some kids downstairs playing," says Baird. (Remember, all of Baird's siblings were upstairs in the radio room with their stepfather). Imagine Baird's reaction when he encountered a little boy he'd never seen before, standing at the foot of the stairs.

"As plain as day—plain as day!" recalls Baird. "He couldn't have been more than six or seven; he was about my age. I remember he had short blond hair and was wearing a long-sleeved shirt with a stripe across the chest. The thing that really sticks out is that the cuff of the shirt was an inch long and it was brown and it was very tattered. I don't know why that sticks out, 'cause I am by no means a fashion critic," he shares with a laugh. "I stood there about five seconds and the kid spoke. 'Come play with me,' he whispered." To say he was shocked would be correct. He was frozen in place. A few seconds later, he realized what he was seeing and reacted accordingly. "I turned around and I ran back upstairs," says Baird. "I never responded."

"I don't think he was there for malice," shares Baird. "I just think he wanted to play." Baird raced to his stepfather's side. "I told my dad, 'There's someone downstairs! There's a kid down there!'" After ten minutes of pestering him, his stepfather trailed downstairs and sure enough there were toys left out, indicating someone had been playing there. Still not convinced it was a ghostly child, he placed the blame on Baird's other brothers and made them clean up the mess, yet again.

As far as Baird knows, none of his brothers actually witnessed an apparition as he had, but each and every one of them clearly remember the perpetual issue with the toys.

Other odd things happened to this family. Baird's childhood involved multiple moves to multiple cities and states. Baird's stepfather had a career that required much travel, so the family was not in one place for very long. The family lived all over Pennsylvania and Ohio, which were within his stepfather's district.

"When we hit Columbus, we moved into a house—ninety percent of the time we rented," says Baird. "It was two days before Thanksgiving. It was the first house we found. We rented it and moved in." From the get go, says Baird, his mom never liked the house. "She would say, 'The house isn't right, I don't know why, but it isn't right.'" Still, there was no choice about leaving. "That was all they had," says Baird, "so we moved in."

"My step dad had to go out of town the day of moving in so he left. Mom was unpacking and one of the bedrooms (the one his brother, Eloy, stayed in) was just cold," recalls Baird, "no matter what she did. She got a space heater and put it in there and it was still cold."

"The whole house would be hot but she could not warm that room up," Baird says. "She went to bed," he says. "The TV came on." His mom yelled at the boys to either turn the TV down or turn it off. The TV stayed on, blaring. His mom went downstairs and nobody was there. Everybody was asleep. She turned it off and went back to bed. The TV would blast back on again. She again came down and saw that a toy with wheels had been left on the stairs. "We got a pretty good talking to," says Baird. "But we didn't do it."

"Every time she would come up or down the stairs, the toy would be back on the stairs—different steps each time. Even if we (the kids) were not in the house at the time, the toy would appear on the stairs."

When his stepfather got home his mother told him, "This ghost is out to hurt me!" Thanksgiving Day came and his mother was cooking dinner. The entire house went dark—all the circuits popped. His mother went downstairs to put them back on; she would get upstairs and they would pop off again. She went down and turned them back on and came back up again, and off they went. She turned the stove off in case that was the trigger. The house still went dark—unless his mother was standing there, watching the fuse box. Then they stayed on. Once she went back upstairs, off they went. His mother had said, "I'm not staying here. I'm not living here. Whatever is here, is out to hurt me."

"The next day we moved across the street," says Baird with a chuckle. "The family that moved in (to the house we'd just left) had kids our age and we all went to the same school. Well, they didn't last long there, either. Mom talked to them and they always agreed that there was something in that house. At nighttime in that room that never got warm, you'd always see lights flickering. They never had a kid sleep in there because they couldn't get it warm. I think they lasted about a month," adds Baird.

An especially tragic and terrifying encounter happened in Baird's family years ago. "I'm thirty-seven," says Baird. "When I was thirteen, my oldest brother died. He was murdered. He was a good kid but he had his issues, especially with alcohol and drugs."

While Baird's mother was at the funeral for her child, a strange woman came forward and told her, "It was always his destiny…to die like this."

"She had never seen this woman before," insists Baird. The unknown woman continued talking and told his mom, "He died just like his father died."

"What do you mean?" Baird's mother asked the woman. "You knew his father?"

"We all know his father," the woman told Baird's mother, then walked away. At the end of the funeral, his mother saw a card lying on the floor and it was from "for lack of a better word, a witchcraft store in Columbus," says Baird. She picked it up.

Curiosity got the better of her and she went to the store to see if she could locate that woman again. "They had a display set up," says

Baird, "and my brother's name, Eloy, a very unique name, was cen-tered in this spiral thing, encased in glass. She never did see the lady. She asked about her; no one would talk to her. She went there with a friend the next day, and that day, a different name was in there."

Baird pauses. "Mom's from Utah," he says. "She left home when she was seventeen and pregnant, and never talked to anyone from her family since." When she finally started talking about it, she told Baird that years ago, when she was a child, Eloy's father had somehow angered a woman in Utah who was known to be a witch and she had told him that there would be some kind of curse would strike down his family and "there will never be a living descendant."

Eloy had one son of the same name and both were murdered at the age of sixteen. Eloy's father had been in a bar fight and killed by a two-by-four to the head and his son, Baird's oldest brother, had been murdered at the same exact age. Was his teenaged brother the victim of his young father's sins; a wicked woman's curse? The mere thought is astonishing and frightening. Baird has been relatively paranormal-free for a while now, and that's admittedly, fine by him.

Chapter 25

The Twilight Man

John Bryan State Park in Yellow Springs

Who is that fellow with the red kerchief around his neck, clad in the blue shirt, and denim overalls hanging out at John Bryan State Park? The man is only witnessed at dusk, strolling out of the west gate, and he is seemingly never in a big hurry, as his left hand is snuggly positioned within the pocket of his jeans. Is he a neighbor, a park visitor, an employee of the park? Not likely, as this particular nighttime visitor always disappears right before he reaches Meredith Road outside the park's entrance.

The Twilight Man has been seen here at the west gate entrance to John Bryan Park, off of Meredith Road.

John Bryan State Park in Yellow Springs, Greene County, Ohio, began in 1896 as "Riverside Farm," an incredibly lush 335-acre tract of land along the Little Miami River gorge. The park exists and is enjoyed by thousands now, all because of the park's namesake. Bryan was a successful entrepreneur who took it upon himself to preserve a good portion of that area as a state preserve. In 1918, Bryan opted to give his beloved Riverside Farm to the state of Ohio as the park's Web site recounts, "To be cultivated by the state as a forestry, botanic and wildlife reserve park and equipment station," and in 1925, it became a state forest park; one of the first, actually.

The DNR took over in 1949, and the U.S. Department of Interior has fittingly designated the park and the abutting Clifton Gorge State Nature Preserve as a National Natural Landmark. There are multiple layers of bedrock; each with its own distinct characteristics from a different time/era. Quaint waterfalls dot the park's landscape, cascading down their rhythmic beauty. With its limestone gorge and incredible flora and fauna (and disappearing fellows) this place is not to be missed by nature lovers and ghost hunters alike.

The plants, trees and shrubs in the park are vast and varied; yes, there are numerous amounts of maples and oaks, but there are also cottonwoods, sycamores, too, in this nature-lover's haven. There are well over 300 species of wildflowers that sprout the landscape and there are numerous species of birds and other wildlife within the grounds, as well. The park offers outdoor sport enthusiasts many options to keep them from every getting bored. There is hiking, rock climbing, biking, camping, fishing, bird watching, and more. It is easy to let your mind and frustrations slip away while navigating the park, or resting beside the banks of the Little Miami River.

If you do visit the park, make sure to keep your eyes open wide in order to take in all of that amazing wildlife and fauna and, of course, for a possible peek at that elusive chap who strolls away from the park at twilight.

John Bryan State Park Campground is located on 3790 State Route 370, Yellow Springs, Ohio, 45387-9743, www. johnbryan.org.

Chapter 26

"Shaker-ing" in his Boots

"In 1983, I partied a lot," admits (writer and jack-of-all trades) J.T. Ryder of Dayton. Ryder currently writes for TourGreatMiami.com a Web site devoted to keeping hip Miami Valley, Ohio, residents up to date on the latest happenings in and around their area.

Prior to this gig, Ryder had lived a life of multiple careers; from cab driver to security officer, and multiple interesting positions in between. While he was younger, however, he devoted himself to having fun, and doing so certainly did not exclude paranormal activity—quite the opposite. One of his more amazing encounters took place at an old Shaker site.

"My friends and I were looking for a place to hang out and party once cold weather hit," Ryder shares. "One day, driving home with my mom (in Kettering, Ohio), I noticed this huge building on the hill. I had seen it hundreds of times before, but now I was seeing it as a potential party palace," he admits with a chuckle. "It was surrounded by two massive barns and some other smaller buildings. I called my friend, (who is now the coach of a major college football team) and told him to meet me at this park that abuts the property. We hooked up there and proceeded to hike up to the main building. It sat atop a hill overlooking everything. I found out later that it was originally a Shaker settlement and that the barns were original structures. (It has since been dismantled and taken to a Shaker museum in Moraine.) It was originally a Shaker farming community before it petered out and the 'congregation' merged with another one farther south.

"Our first visit there was filled with more feelings then actual events," Ryder shares. Subsequent visits, however, revealed more. Much, much more.

"Weather" You Believe This or Not...

Ryder does not deny that he and his friends were frequenting the place in order to have a couple of brews, but that pastime cannot completely explain away what he and his buddies witnessed on that incredible parcel of land. Bringing the weather indoors is a figurative saying, unless you were Ryder years ago in that old Shaker barn.

While the group was inside one of the structures, nature's fury erupted.

"It was raining inside (the barn) and a flood of water was cascading down the stairwell," recalls Ryder. Was this simply a case of the roof leaking and letting in the weather outside? No, not possible, says Ryder, because it wasn't raining at all outside. It was only raining inside. Was this a means for the devoutly religious people who had passed on to let Ryder and his buddies know they did not approve of their beer drinking? Possibly. According to Ryder, that grassy hill and the buildings upon it were a cornucopia of paranormal anomalies.

Another time, in that same barn, the young men all bore witness to a faceless vision. "It was a glowing figure with no features," says Ryder. "It was wearing what struck me as bishops' robes. It was standing stationary at the top of the stairs.

"Figures (apparitions) could be seen by many (at one time, there was a group of six of us going on a nighttime investigation) in the field, marking our movements." These specters were following the young men, seeming to chronicle their activities.

On a more personal level, Ryder witnessed a remarkable greeting of sorts from beyond. "My name appeared carved in the doorway of another one of the structures," he says. It just appeared out of nowhere. This was a sobering message for the partying fellow to be sure.

"Here is the weirdest thing about the place," shares Ryder. "It was situated between two of the biggest party plats in Kettering, yet there were no beer bottles, smashed-out windows, nor graffiti...none of the signs of teenagers taking up occupancy were there. When I say it was close, it was just a cornfield away from these plats. Even the field tools remained untouched in the basement with shelves of seeds lining the walls."

Even after the structure was leveled, the barns moved, and a research park developed on the site, the land still held a weird fascination for Ryder. Turns out there was a Shaker cemetery that was unearthed during excavation, and there is now a marker of this alongside the road.

According to Ryder, the building that was erected over the site of the original building still has "issues" for employees and maintenance workers. Maybe not so much today, with all of the development around there, he admits, but even into the late nineties, when he was an alarm investigator, "employees would tell me of seeing shadows moving, lights constantly blowing out, elevators starting and stopping themselves," he says. A memorial to the Watervliet Shakers is erected at the corner of what was once Patterson Road and County Line Road. According to Ryder, the area still retains recognition of its Shaker roots because Patterson Road turns into Shakertown Road.

The memorial for the Watervliet Shakers in Dayton.

Chapter 27

Sensing the Unseen: Staci Calden

There Goes George Again!

Staci Calden is familiar with the paranormal. No, she does not belong to a ghost hunting group, nor does she have any particular interest in the subject. She is one of those people where the paranormal has found her and not let go. For one thing, she is a psychic. For another, she has had experiences in Miamisburg, Ohio, at her father's old house in Germantown, Ohio, and in Tennessee.

"I really believe Central Avenue in Miamisburg is a haunted street," she says. "Several of the houses of people who have lived there have stories. My story was on Central Avenue in the early 2000s. I was in my dad's house. Back then, he had the old heaters that came out of the floor, and he had ceiling fans, and in his dining room was a half bath." One day, Calden recalls stopping at the house to use the restroom. While doing so, she noticed that the tablecloth was swaying mightily. Calden figured it was the cat playing around, but still she wondered how the feline was able to get it to sway so much. When she walked out of the bathroom, she saw the cat lounging by the door; yet the swaying continued. What was causing the tablecloth to move so much? She has no clue to this day.

"I left," says Calden, "I didn't want to stick around and see why it was doing it. It was too weird. It kept doing it until I left. I was creeped out," admits Calden. "That house has always been creepy."

She recalls being there one night alone with her boyfriend when they heard someone (something?) race down the stairs. They both looked up and down the staircase, says Calden. "No one was there."

Calden has also heard a train and felt its vibration passing by the house while in the basement; even though there was no train passing at the time. Turns out Calden had company when it came to admitting that something paranormal was going on.

"My dad named his ghost, George," says Calden. "Nobody wanted to go in the room that was mine (for every other weekend). My sister said 'There's a scary man in there,'" recalls Calden. "It always felt so cold and the closet really bothered me," she adds.

Calden's father talked about paranormal things happening all the time, she says. He would hear noises and would talk a lot about "people" laughing in the hallways when he was alone in the house.

Cheerio! London Street in Dayton Ohio

When Calden was about ten or eleven years old, she was beginning to realize that she might have inherent psychic tendencies. One October day, while Calden was in sixth grade, she was visiting her friend in her family's house on London Avenue in Dayton. "Her kitchen was so heavy, I couldn't breathe in there," Calden recalls. That kitchen was such an issue for her that she would do her best to avoid being in there. She says she would take "the long way" to get to bedrooms instead of simply strolling through the kitchen.

One day her friend's family was outside hanging up Christmas lights and, in a rare situation to be sure, Calden found herself in the kitchen alone eating a piece of hard cinnamon candy.

"It got stuck in my throat and I started choking," says Calden. "I didn't run out to get them; I don't know why. I just stood in this kitchen, and I just kind of froze. I ended up going over to the sink, and I don't know how that happened. I never would have known enough to go lean over the sink (I don't know if someone pushed me) in order to get something out of me, but something for some reason made me lean over the sink. The candy dislodged out of my throat.

"I remember thinking afterwards, 'Maybe this heaviness in the kitchen is not a bad thing,'" quips Calden. After all, whatever was creating that heaviness just might have saved her life.

Auf Weidersehen Ghosts

In August of 1994, Calden was at her sister's home in Germantown, Ohio, rocking her newborn nephew to lull him to sleep. It was dark, as only midnight could be, and Calden's boyfriend was sleeping on the couch beside them. "All of the sudden, the faucet in the kitchen went on full-blast," she recalls. "I had to turn that faucet off and I'm like, 'Wow, what is with this place?'"

According to Calden, Germantown is another one of those haunted cities, overall. The mound is in between those two cities where they have all that nuclear waste, and there's an Indian mound that's across the street from there. Calden's aunt lives close by, and there is a section of her subdivision that they will not build upon. "I've been taught that where there's new developments, it's typical to see ghosts," Calden notes.

Although the following experience for this Ohio woman happened several states south, she said it was one of the more terrifying paranormal experiences she's ever had. It was while she was on vacation in the mountains in a newly built cabin in Pigeon Forge, Tennessee, in 2005, that Calden experienced one of the most frightening events of her life.

Calden and her extended family were all staying at a brand-spanking-new cabin. "We were in bed, (her young son was in the room with her) and I had just fallen asleep, and I felt like there was somebody in that room. Well, I thought it could be animals…nothing. It stopped. Then it happened again. My son had woken up and I'd gotten him back asleep (my husband, who had been sleeping on the couch due to his snoring) came into the room and said, 'You okay?'"

Calden told him she was fine and her husband returned to saw some z's on the couch. It wasn't too long before she detected a sound at the door, so she called out her husband's name. There was no response.

"I laid back down and I (felt something walk in). I thought my husband had come back into the room to see if the baby was okay. I went back to sleep and all of the sudden I felt somebody was right next to the bed. I felt the walking and heard the walking," she expounds. "I kept hearing footsteps in the room. I kept trying to come up with different scenarios, but they didn't jive." Calden pauses for a moment.

"You can feel when people are on top of you, you know? You can just tell," says Calden, "and that's when I wigged out." She screamed for her husband, who came rushing in to the bedroom.

"There's somebody in here; but they're not in here! I don't know how to explain it," blubbered Calden. Her husband was saying things like, "Okay, it's okay."

"My Dad woke up, everybody in the cabin woke up. I'm sure everybody on the mountain woke up. I was so loud," admits Calden with a laugh. Only her husband knew what really had happened because Calden didn't want to upset the rest of the family; especially her young nephews.

"We were up the next night and my dad and my sister talked about how they had heard the pool table being used (it hadn't been used by live individuals, however). They didn't know about my experience then either," says Calden. The vacation then continued without any more major paranormal incidences. What amazed Calden was what happened once they'd returned home to Ohio.

After the family vacation had ended, she received a call from her stepmother, saying, "You've got to see this!" It should be noted that her stepmother was not a believer in ghosts or the paranormal. Yet, she could not dispel what she was seeing: Apparently, nestled within the traditional, family-fun photos that she'd taken, was a particularly interesting picture. It showed the image of a ghostly apparition in the cabin. "He was wearing suspenders and what looked like a Civil War era hat," says Calden. "I felt like he was evil and hateful and scary (when he was in the bedroom with us that night) and when I looked at him, that's exactly like I felt." This ghost was obviously not one of the happy/Casper variety. Frankly, he looked downright vicious.

"I slept with a night light for a while. It took me a good week to get over that. It was awful," says Calden. How was it that her intuitive radar kicked into high gear that night at the cabin?

"Throughout my whole life, I would know things," explains Calden. "I would know things like when my grandparents were gonna die…it was just strange. It's almost like I had a dream, but I wasn't sleeping. Even now, I get a lot of information at nighttime. I had this vision of them dying in their casket when I'm lying on my bed." [Her Grandpa] died of a heart attack, so there was no warning, but Calden felt it [envisioned it] regardless.

In 2005, Calden accompanied her aunt to a psychic. The psychic told Calden that she was not only extremely psychic but also extremely advanced. "All my life I thought, 'Oh, you're just imagining this,' or thought it was just normal. If I'm at Wal-Mart and some lady walks in, it's almost like I created her life in my head. I knew you just drank last night, your dad is doing this. I just thought it was normal or that I was assuming things about them."

Calden has worked to hone in on her psychic abilities by getting pointers from a psychic that tutors her. When family members' items come up missing; often Calden is the first person they call.

"I've learned how to clear my head (and it's actually like a fishbowl, a clear, round fishbowl with water in it) and I lose all the water in my mind and whatever appears first that's how I know where it is."

Help My Baby!

"A year ago, I had a dream where I felt like I was a video camera in this room and a little girl was crying and crying. She cried forever." A woman (deceased) came to Calden and told her: "Help my baby, help my baby. Somebody's got to help my baby!"

"She was showing me this bed from the 1970s and telling me that somebody was hurting her child in her bedroom at night. It was dark. That is one of the times where I had somebody come to me when she was dead." The identity of the child was instinctively known by Calden, although she did not see her face in the vision and it was later revealed to her who this girl was and that this poor little girl had been sexually molested by a relative's boyfriend.

"It wore me out. It wears me down. It's almost like she was laying on me to tell me," says Calden. "I don't have to see dead people," says Calden. "That's a choice." If Calden is not up to it, she will refuse to deal with it. "I just say out loud, 'Nope, go away.'"

Calden has considered eventually doing readings for people, but is still in the beginning stages of getting her psychic feet grounded and confident. "[The psychic] has taught me so much," she shares.

This woman is visited by spirits on a regular basis, she shares, and that can certainly be disconcerting. She's working hard at dealing with her psychic abilities in the best manner possible.

"I can't choose who will come around, but I can choose who I will listen to. I don't like to be bothered in the flesh," says Calden. "She now tells any entities that might be around her not to touch her, nor scare her. "It's finally worked because I've become confident with it."

Chapter 28

The Witch's Tower

The Witch's Tower in Kettering, Ohio, is a looming site many don't see every day. Well, that is unless they happen to live in the neighborhood or commonly shoot eighteen holes at the Dayton Community Golf course it overlooks. "I've heard all sorts of stories about it," says J.T. Ryder, "but nobody knows why it was built or even who built it." It rests on the Patterson homestead land. To build a structure like that for surveying one location seems a little excessive, Ryder muses. Many groups (professional and amateur) have investigated the site over the years with varying results. Some years ago, the tower was sealed off to guard against rampant vandalism.

The Haunted Investigators team which consists of Christopher Bores, Alan Cicco, and Jennifer Shippel were at the site in 2007, and although the interior was already sealed off, they concentrated their studies on the outside area of the structure. It is a tall stone tower with a turret on the top; it looks like a mini castle. The tower has held numerous titles, including being called Patterson Tower, the Witch's Tower, the Tower of Doom, and even Frankenstein's Castle. Its sky-high tower has a murky past that nobody seems to be able to get to the bottom of.

The impressive structure stands six stories high and looms forebodingly on the crest of a hilltop. It is speculated that the tower was erected in the 1800s and used as a lookout tower during the Civil War, notes Bores. It's also been rumored that a woman in the early 1900s leaped off the turret of the tower, plunging to her death. More recently, the legend hints that several teenagers met their demise at the site during a thunderstorm when they were unlucky enough to be leaning against the tower's railing and were hit by lightning and instantly killed.

Ryder was up there many times as a teenager before the tower was sealed off. Every high school has a story about a teenager going out there and getting struck by lightning, says Ryder, adding that he believes that is one of the urban legends. "Nobody that I know of has

The Witch's (Patterson) Tower.

The rear view of the Witch's Tower.

actually died there," says Ryder. "It was a very hot spot for teenagers for many years," he notes, "as it was creepy, cool, and romantic all at the same time." It's been said that a figure in a long, black robe haunts the structure at night and can sometimes be seen peeking down over the turret to the landscape below.

"I almost got pushed off of it," shares Ryder, but not by a ghost. "This was one of my practical jokes gone awry. Everybody that came to the tower did the same thing," says Ryder. "They climb up the stairs, walk to the front, and look out. You can see everything."

The teen was standing up there and the girl he was dating at the time arrived to meet him, and he popped up, surprising her. So much so that she gave him a hearty shove, which almost sent him flying over the top of the turret. That is about the only factual evidence he knows of somebody almost dying there, he shares with a laugh.

Still, the inkling that somebody perished there at one time or another will not die. During their investigation, the Haunted Investigators crew did not capture any EVPs or photograph any anomalies while at the site, but the video camera that Bores was using that night turned off and/ or paused repeatedly without anybody touching it. The batteries were freshly charged and they cannot come up with a sound reason for this to have occurred, he notes. Given that, Bores believes it is indeed "plausible" that a spirit of some sort is in the area.

Regardless, it certainly looks like the perfect locale for a specter to hang out, and that makes it all the more fun to visit.

The Witch's Tower is located overlooking Dayton's Community Golf Course on Patterson Avenue in Kettering, Ohio.

Chapter 29

The Patterson Homestead

The Patterson Homestead Historic House Museum has a welcoming vibe from every angle. The three-story, white brick house looms in the midst of a fine neighborhood and has been beckoning museum-goers for over thirty years. It was originally the home of Colonel Robert Patterson, his wife, Elizabeth, and subsequent generations (the Patterson name is an important one in Dayton history and sprinkled throughout this book).

The house was built in three components from 1810 to 1850. Numerous children were born and lived in the house.

The Patterson Homestead.

In 1884, brothers John H. and Frank J. Patterson founded the National Cash Register Company; their factory eventually erected on the north side of the family's farm acreage. In 1953, the house (including all of its incredible antique furnishings) and its eight and a half acres was bestowed to the City of Dayton to be utilized as a family memorial and meeting center. It has been widely theorized by many that the Patterson Homestead has regular visitors from beyond.

It is said that the Patterson farmhouse is home to several entities, and yes, it is believed that at least one of them is a member of the Patterson family, since he's witnessed in military garb ascending to the top floor (which is not open to museum-goers).

The peals of phantom children-at-play are sometimes heard, their laughter echoing down the farmhouse halls. Volunteers have been teased periodically by an unseen force that finds it amusing to fling gingerbread men off the line they were drying on, or to lock them out of a room. There is a breeze within the home that does not seem to be generated from heating or cooling units, and it moves throughout the structure.

Eric Bolin, who is an investigator with the Ohio Paranormal Exploration Society (OPES), as well as Southern Director for TOP-org, has investigated the paranormal with several groups, most recently with OPES. Bolin investigated the Patterson Homestead multiple times and truly believes, given his (and his fellow investigators') experiences and data collected that this place is haunted.

"The night was October 12th, 2006," says Bolin. "We arrived at Patterson Homestead in an attempt to prove or disprove years of reports of paranormal activity at the historical farmhouse. We arrived around 9 pm, and all was quiet for the majority of the night. Around approximately 11:30 pm, I was standing in the doorway of the second-floor master bedroom. To the left of the door is an old travel desk that once belonged to Jefferson Patterson. Alongside of the desk was the bed, and at the foot of the bed was an old Patterson family crib. I turned to my left and proceeded to take a picture of the travel desk. After the picture was taken, I turned to my right and standing between myself and the crib, no more than two feet away, was the figure of a man with arms to his side. He was just staring at me. He was gone in three seconds.

"Around 1 am, as we were leaving for the night, one of my members, Paul, went into the front yard to take an exterior photo for the website. The only other people present were myself and the museum director. The director was locking up from the outside, and I was right beside her. The house was empty. Upon reviewing

Dark figure in the Patterson front window. *Courtesy of Paul Johnston Jr.*

photos, Paul lightened one photo up and noticed something 'odd.' After zooming in on the window, he noticed a black figure standing at the window. This was the window to the same room where I saw the apparition. (The apparition) was looking out the window. Upon looking at a brochure I picked up that night at the museum, I saw a picture of a man with a full beard, and immediately remembered the face. It was Jefferson Patterson, the man who was staring at me the night before."

The museum is certainly worth a visit regardless of whether you are lucky enough to catch a glimpse of Mr. Patterson or not.

The Patterson Homestead Historic House Museum is located at: 1815 Brown Street in Dayton, Ohio 45409. Eric can be reached at eric@top-org.net. Web site: www.daytonhistory.org/patt_home_htm.

Chapter 30

Lizzie's Story

"I saw your posting and knew I had to tell our story," says Lizzie of Dayton. "In the fall of 1998, I moved my family into a home on Kenilworth Avenue, a beautiful large double. The very first night there it began. As my husband and I lay sleeping, a strange sensation came over my husband. He woke up feeling like he was being held down, only to find not a person but a 'cloud' over him. He described the cloud as being very dark with no clear edges. He was unable to speak or move to awaken me. This went on only a minute or two and then the cloud spiraled toward the ceiling and was gone. He was then able to wake me, tell me what had happened, and was unable to return to sleep for several hours." What a housewarming, eh?

"The next morning," says Lizzie, "we decided not to tell the children what had happened." They didn't want to alarm their youngsters and hoped that the strange "cloud" was a one-time thing.

"Several nights later, my daughter, who was fourteen at that time, came to our bedroom, asking about a noise she was hearing," says Lizzie. "We did not hear it but she was positive there was something in the attic making a noise like a ball being rolled and bounced. I then went to her closet where the walk-up attic was located." Lizzie ascended the stairs to take a look.

"When I entered the attic I saw nothing," she notes, "but I felt very strange. Not scared, just strange. I reassured my daughter there was nothing wrong and told her to go back to bed. When I returned to my bed, I told my husband how I felt up there. He said he had not felt afraid on our first night either, just a strange feeling. He insisted that our new home was haunted. I laughed at him and said, 'I just hope the ghost is friendly.'"

The couple was starting to think they really might have something paranormal going on, but neither of them wanted to truly believe it was so. "The next morning, my daughter said that as soon as I had left her room, the noise started again, and she listened to it for most of the night, unable to sleep." Her daughter told her mother that the sounds didn't scare her, but they did bother her, nonetheless. "This happened many more times while we lived there," says Lizzie.

The family went on with their lives, mentally making note of the odd occurrences, but also learning how to live with them. "A few weeks later, my daughter was dog-sitting for her grandpa. When the dog entered my bedroom," says Lizzie, "her eyes fixed on a corner of the ceiling and she began barking furiously. Nothing could calm her down and this went on all weekend with the dog whining and scratching at my closed door."

"My youngest son was just eight, but had never been afraid of much," she continues. At least not until the family had moved into the beautiful house in Dayton. "He would not enter any of the three levels of the house unless someone was with him," recalls Lizzie. "He said that he felt like someone else was there.

"I told him it was just his imagination but he never relented the whole time we lived there." Her boy had definitely felt that something was in that house; something he couldn't see that was watching him.

The holidays were not a time of paranormal respite, either, no matter how much the family would have appreciated the break. "Just days before Thanksgiving, my best friend and I were baking pies," says Lizzie. "I had shut off my mixer and my friend said to beat the batter longer. After a few times of beating away, I told her it was done, but she insisted that it wasn't." Well, her friend had an invisible ally that day because, "my mixer turned right back on! Needless to say, I mixed longer," she quips. "This particular event caused me to really think that my home was haunted."

Lizzie felt that she couldn't deny that odd events were happening much longer...it was getting very blatant. "Later on that season, I talked with my neighbor lady, feeling foolish asking whether there were any bizarre incidents happening on her property," says Lizzie, "but she said there was nothing strange going on (at her house)." Great. The paranormal "fun" seemed to be centered on Lizzie's house alone.

"Very often we would catch a glimpse of a person-type shape out of the corners of our eyes," notes Lizzie, "but never a clear image.

"Another very strange thing happened often in our kitchen," she adds. "There was this loud swooshing sound coming from inside our fridge. We would joke that the ghost was stuck in there since all we had to do was open the door, close it back, and the sound was gone," she says.

There were other interesting phenomena for the family to witness throughout the years. They certainly didn't get bored! "We came home one night to (our empty house) to see a blue light shining from our attic window," she says. "My husband went into the house, leaving me and the kids in the car. The light went off as soon as he opened the front door. He went to the attic, and saw nothing," she says, "but he had that same, strange feeling. After several months of weirdness, we just accepted the house as being haunted.

In the spring, my neighbor went to a new beautician. As they were talking, the conversation turned to our neighborhood. The beautician told my neighbor she had lived in our block at Kenilworth when she was a child. She then told my neighbor about the old lady who had died in the double across the street from her (our house). She had lived alone and had not been found for several days after her death. She couldn't remember which side the lady had lived on but my neighbor was sure which one. She was at my door as soon as she got home, telling me what she had just learned.

"I was not at all surprised," says Lizzie. "I somehow knew our ghost was female. I told our ghost out loud that I was glad she was nice to us and not harming my children. I told her not to be afraid of us, as we were not afraid of her. By this time, my sons knew what was happening, and even though I assured them she was nice, my youngest still never entered a level that was unoccupied, at least by the living.

"When it came time to move out a couple years later, two friends of my husband's were carrying a wardrobe down the steps when one of them saw her image. The wardrobe was dropped, the friend ran out the door screaming, and would not return to the house. The other man did not see her image, but was sure from his friend's action and pale color that he had indeed seen a ghost. We lost both guys at that point. As the last of the boxes were finally out, I said goodbye to our ghost, again thanking her for never harming my family."

Chapter 31

The Forgotten Dead... Remembered

The Universalist Cemetery in Springboro Ohio

A cemetery that has certainly seen better days lies cloaked behind a booming tire store—its presence unknown for years to many.

"The cemetery is about 200 years old and it was built behind what used to be a Universalist Church in Springboro, Ohio," shares Penny Massie, historian and DGHS investigator. "It had been abandoned. Springboro police didn't even know it was there. It is in bad condition from being left for all of these years."

DGHS President Robin Albright expounds, "As a service project, our group has 'adopted' this old cemetery in Springboro. We have

Universalist Cemetery in Springboro. *Courtesy of Javier Perez*

been coordinating with the Historical Society in this effort. DGHS has been involved in clearing brush, dead wood, trash, etc., to make way for a fence to be installed around the perimeter. The fence has now been installed by Springboro and we are beginning our spring cleanup. The next phase will be additional research, landscaping, etc. As with many small, old cemeteries, many of those interred are children and most of the stones are broken. Efforts are being made to accord this final resting place the dignity it deserves.

"It needs quite a bit of work," notes Massie. "Our group goes in and tries to do monthly cleanups." Massie adds that they will "eventually try and restore the tombstones, plant flowers, and add benches to make this place even more beautiful." While undertaking this process, several of those affiliated with DGHS have had some interesting events occur while working to revive the once forgotten cemetery.

The grave of Sarah at Universalist Cemetery. *Courtesy of Javier Perez*

"Other members have had experiences during cleanups at this site. I feel very peaceful when I'm here," Massie says. "There is a tombstone that has the name Sarah on it that there have been many stories about. It seems that when you place the stone in the base, it eventually gets laid on the ground, face-up yet at a diagonal from the base. If it had fallen, there would have been no way for it to land like this. I did set it up, but couldn't get it to move while I was there. But, I left and came back one time and the stone was back on the ground in the same position." Massie admits that someone else could have moved it, but it is odd, nonetheless.

"I would have to personally see it move to be sure that it was a ghost who moved it," she says. "I did, however, get an EVP (electronic voice phenomenon) not too far from the stone," notes Massie. "It seems to be saying, 'This is Mary's tomb (pause) stone.' Maybe it is possible that this isn't Sarah's tombstone, but Mary's. There are other tombstones that do say Mary on them. Who knows for sure?" Massie adds.

"My son was with me one day helping me clean (the cemetery) and he claimed to have heard a little girl's voice from the back/left of the cemetery. He continued to work, and then all of a sudden, became pale and said that there was something evil there. He really became upset and wanted to leave," Massie notes. "Then another lady came into the cemetery from the group, and all of a sudden, his evil feeling went away. He came back to himself and went back to work. I never understood what had happened to him."

Jim has been an investigator with DGHS for over four years. He became interested in the group after discussing paranormal things with Robin Albright, the founder. He noticed something quite interesting while working at the cemetery in the summer of 2007.

"It was at the edge of the cemetery we were restoring," says Jim. He witnessed the figure of a girl, watching the group. "She was about average size with long straight dark red hair. She was wearing a smock-like red dress. It had an off-white plaque with embroidery. There may also have been a boy with her about the same age or younger, white shirt, sleeves rolled up, blue overalls, dark bowl-cut hair. He is the only child of several playing in their house's back yard that at least minimally interacted with the girl. He stood beside her a couple of times, then ran off to play with the other kids."

Jim recalls, "The girl stood and watched us work for a couple of hours. She was standing in a tunnel through the underbrush on the eastern side of the cemetery. The tunnel was about six feet wide, and about seven or eight high, and was in line with the patio doors of the house behind us. She stood in the twilight area of the tunnel at the end away from the cemetery." According to the DGHS investigator, the girl had a neutral expression on her face the entire time.

What's interesting is that this man was not working clean up alone in the cemetery that day. "Since the girl had stood there for a couple of hours watching us work, I asked several of the party if they had seen her," he says. "None said they had."

Jim will probably continue his association with DGHS because he is intrigued with the process. "I would be interested in finding out what, if anything, we are actually seeing," he says. "Most of my 'sightings' have been much like this. Usually in broad daylight, there was nothing to indicate anything out of the ordinary except a lack of interaction, from the other kids who were playing out, or people that were going about their daily business."

It's nice to know that people, such as DGHS, care enough to undertake such a work-intensive project; and look out for the tombstones and land which is the final resting place for those who so long ago passed away. Perhaps the little girl is showing herself as a way of thanking the group for fixing up her digs.

Chapter 32

The Haunted Apartaments

"Back in 1993 to 1996, my ex and I lived at 10 El Morado Place in Dayton," shares Tana Nichols. "I think it was Apartment #2 and also Apartment #4, which happened to be side by side." Nichols, who now resides in Michigan, cannot get the time spent in those apartments out of her mind; and for good reason.

"One afternoon in Apartment #4, I was talking to a friend on the phone, and heard my 'ex' doing dishes," says Nichols. "I had my back to the front door, and thought he had gotten home early from work. I said goodbye, and called out, 'Hi, honey, I didn't hear you come in,' as I walked into the kitchen. I was quite surprised when I saw no one was in the kitchen," she adds. Turns out Nichol's husband arrived home about twenty minutes later.

"This kitchen was directly across from the other kitchen in Apartment #2, which at the time, was unoccupied," Nichols notes. "Well, a year later, we moved into that apartment; it had two bedrooms and was huge. Around 3 am one morning, we were awoken by the sound of breaking glass coming from the kitchen. We knew immediately that someone was in the apartment. I grabbed the phone and called 911. As I talked to the dispatcher, we could hear someone going through the cupboard drawers, like they were looking for something. The sounds were very loud, and our bedroom was a room away from the kitchen. The back door to the apartment, which was in the kitchen, had a four pane window in it, so the sound that woke us up was that window being broken, or so we thought! It was very loud, and we heard distinct movement before the sounds of drawers being rummaged through."

"At one point my ex hollered, 'Get out of here! The cops are coming!' and when this happened the dispatcher told us to 'be quiet so they don't coming looking for you.' I told her that we were hearing them going through the drawers and cupboards. Then, after about four minutes, the sound stopped. When she told us it was okay to go downstairs, I was really surprised, because we did not hear anyone running out the door, or the police shouting halt, etc. I was afraid to leave the bedroom, because the police were outside, and not in our kitchen where I thought they should be!"

The couple reiterated the frightening scenario to the officers. "The police said that it was the storm door banging in the wind," Nichols shares. "I can assure you that it was not a storm door in the wind."

Despite knowing darn well that the door was not the sound they heard, the couple had no choice but to let it slide and the police departed. "We still had that disoriented feeling you get when the fire alarm goes off and you're asleep," says Nichols. "We went in the kitchen, and I thought maybe the spice rack on the wall had fallen, but not a thing was out of place. We went back to bed scratching our heads and it wasn't until a couple of weeks later that I put the two stories (the dish washing sounds in the other kitchen and this one) together. I tried slamming the storm door, but it had one of those door stoppers that prevented it from slamming and making a noise." Too bad they hadn't noticed that fact when the police were there.

"Another time, I was coming out of the bedroom into the living room, and thought I saw a little white dog run through," says Nichols. There were other oddities, as well. "I sometimes would get a kind of feeling of despair when I was alone. I never really felt afraid, just really sad a lot," she says.

There was an issue for Nichols with a piece of furniture, as well. "We had an old rocking chair I bought at a thrift store, and even before the above incident, I always thought I was going to wake up and see if rocking by itself." The feeling that it would happen was very strong. "Maybe that sounds weird," admits Nichols, "but this chair really scared me after I brought it home. I tried not to look at it when I was alone. I thought I was just being silly, and maybe I was, but I have not had that type of reaction since.

"We later moved out of the building (not because it was haunted, but due to another issue) and a friend moved into this apartment right after us. While we lived there, we had a cat who didn't seem to have a problem with the apartment," admits Nichols, "but his cat refused to go in the kitchen, and had to be fed in the living room. The first thing their friend told them upon seeing them was, 'That apartment is weird!'

"I have often thought about trying to contact the present occupant to see if they had any experiences, without telling them mine first," she says. "I heard about other things happening in the apartment building also. I think it was built around 1920 in the Spanish Villa style. It is located by the Dayton Art Institute. A neighbor who lived on their street, asked us if we knew any weird stories, because she had heard some things about strange noises in the place," notes Nichols. "It was after that when I started putting the incidents together."

As to whether odd events are still happening in El Morado, only the latest residents would know for sure.

The El Morado Place Apartments in Dayton.

Chapter 33

Life-long Hauntings

"I have been visited by or had ghosts around me all of my life," says Susan Spradlin, who lives in a rural Dayton-area town. "When I was a child, we lived in a place that used to be military barracks and they rented them out as apartments, and we moved in there. At night, there was something that would come into our bedroom. It was a dark shadow. My brother was always fighting it. We would pull our covers up, cover our heads, and it would pull our covers off."

Having an unknown/unseeable entity pull one's bed covers off of them would be disconcerting to an adult, let alone young children.

Yes, the parents of five children knew that it was happening, says Spradlin, "But there was nothing they could do. That really scared me. I was too young to understand what was going on. We were poor; we had nothing. We couldn't move, we had to stay where we were."

Eventually, the family was able to move to a house that was converted to a duplex in the area but, believe it or not, that didn't turn out to be much better—at least not on the paranormal front.

Her family heard footsteps on the stairs just about daily; often at the same times. "There were five of us kids," says Spradlin. "And we all remember. He always displayed activity. He would drop things and make noises."

One Thanksgiving the family was just getting ready to sit down to eat their feast and "we heard somebody coming down the stairs. Step, step, step, step..." Spradlin notes. "Everybody heard it. He (the ghost) was not shy at all." It was then when Spradlin's father put his foot down.

"That is enough!" said her dad, referring to the uninvited paranormal party crasher. "I've had it! That SOB is not going to mess up our Thanksgiving dinner!"

Her father flung open that door to the other portion of the house and yelled upstairs: "Listen here: If you want to come down and have dinner with us, you can. Otherwise, get yourself upstairs and be quiet! I am not putting up with (this racket), this year!"

"He (the ghost) was quiet for the rest of the night," shares Spradlin with a grin. Spradlin's siblings knew what was going on and had their own experiences to back it up.

"The duplex wasn't rented at the time," says Spradlin's sister, Jenny Woodworth. "But it seemed like about four o'clock every afternoon you could hear somebody unlock the door, come in, walk up the steps, and then go into the bedroom. We always heard one shoe drop," Woodworth notes. "Really?" interjects Spradlin. "I heard two!" Regardless, the women agree with all of the other aspects.

"He would go across to the bathroom and come back to the bedroom and lay down," Woodworth continues. "The same routine over and over."

Although they did learn to live with it/him, because they had no choice, it wasn't easy for a child to live in a home with such an active ghost.

"I would stay at the front door (at that time of day) because my mom was working," Woodworth notes, adding that she was ever poised to race out that door should the need arise.

"We found out later that someone had committed suicide up there," she adds. "The man had killed himself over the loss of a woman," Spradlin adds. Woodworth was about nine years old at the time and Spradlin was about four.

According to the two siblings, all five kids recall that ghost. "My brother and I used to go upstairs and play up there," notes Spradlin. "There was an attic access at the top of the stairs and we would go up in there and play hide 'n seek. He locked me in and someone touched me. I was crying and screaming, 'Let me out!'"

Spradlin's entire clan knew that this paranormal "man" was hanging out in the upstairs portion of their house and there was little they could do about it. Frustrating to be sure. They all coexisted as best as they could until they moved.As we hear so often in these accounts, moving did not put an end to these two women's paranormal encounters. It seems that once that elusive door has been cracked open, it's very difficult to keep it closed; no matter where you live.

"We had a house in Arcana that was definitely haunted," says Woodworth, adding that it was her daughter who caught the brunt of the ghostly antics.

"Her radio would turn on by itself or the radio station would change channels by itself," she recalls. The TV would come on, the lights would flash off and on, the doorbell would ring by itself, and one day, she saw a man all dressed in black. He walked into another room and disappeared into the wall. This happened just a few months before her grandmother died and they wonder if the man in black might have been a harbinger of her impending death.

Seems the women have a gift of foretelling the future that may have been passed down in the family.

"Before the Xenia tornado came, I had had the dream about that tornado three times," says Spradlin. "I've had one dream besides that twice. It's where we are being attacked and there is a soldier that is rescuing me and we are running into the school in Fairborn (designated shelter). When I was probably fifteen, when I had it the first time, and within a couple of years I had it the second time, but I haven't had it since. I thought, 'That's weird, why would a soldier be saving me?' My mom was there and we were having trouble trying to get in there. I've since learned that the school is one of the designated shelter areas here." [[**How scary is this....**]]

Woodworth had a repeated dream about a tornado, as well and one did strike Arcana.

"My most recent encounter was around this time last year," shares Spradlin. "I live in an area Indians used to travel through. I saw a soldier dressed in gray. I was out at the barn and I had just finished feeding the horses and I was standing by the gate looking into the field. I went, 'Hey! What's that guy doing in my field? Are there more? Are they doing a reenactment?'"

She looked away for a second and he was gone. "It was a ghost!" she shares, her eyes glistening at the memory. "He was holding what appeared to be a sword in his right hand. He had a belt on and gray pants and one of those square-type caps. The shirt or jacket he was wearing was longer; mid-thigh. His pants had a stripe down the leg." According to the energetic blond woman, the solider "was holding (the gun/sword) outward in front of him as he walked across my back pasture.

"That same night, after I saw the solider, I was back out at the barn and I was standing there in front of the door and a rock was thrown at me and it landed in the gravel," she says. Spradlin wondered who/what had thrown the rock toward her—and truth be told she still does. She admittedly has no clue who or what tossed it in her direction, but it was enough to send her running into the house to tell her husband.

Months later, they were having excavations done on their property and Spradlin was outside taking photos of their land so she could email them to her husband (who was serving one of his tours in Iraq as a 1st Sergeant in the U.S. Army). She sent them off and thought nothing of it until she was gathering information for her interview for this book. While she and some others were looking through her photos, they spotted a blue, diamond shape hovering above the spot where the phantom soldier had been seen. There are three photos that have

The back field of Susan Spradlin's property.

Blue diamond shapes appeared in several photos Spradlin
took after sighting the phantom soldier on her acreage.
Courtesy of Susan Spradlin

this diamond shape; one containing multiple diamond images; not all were taken the same day. The same camera took other photos that day that have no diamond shapes, so it couldn't have been a mark on the camera lens. One of the photos actually has several diamonds; one of which is blue, the other two diamond shapes appear as vague, white outlines.

"I noticed that the first two were taken on June 20, 2007," says Spradlin, "and the last one was taken on June 21, 2007. The diamond is in those three pictures but none of the others I took those same days from different directions," she adds.

That is not the only strange sighting at her current home, either. "My daughter was here visiting me from Texas this past July," says Spradlin. "She was sitting on my couch in the living room when she saw a man walk into our den with his head down like he was reading a book." Her daughter noted that the fellow looked just like Spradlin's husband. 'Mom, I saw a man,' her daughter whispered. 'He looked like he was about Tim's height and he had his head down like he was reading a book.'

"My husband is an avid reader," says Spradlin. "He reads constantly. I ran to confront this man," Spradlin says, "however the door was still closed and when it was opened, there was nobody there."

Her husband was in Iraq at this time and the sighting unnerved Spradlin and her daughter greatly. Fearing that her husband might have been injured or killed and that her daughter saw his spirit, it was especially traumatizing. Thankfully, her husband called her a few hours after the sighting, so she knew everything was a-okay. Spradlin says that her daughter, who has MS has noticed a correlation between an increase in her MS symptoms and her awareness of potential paranormal activity around her. The intuitive lineage is alive and well.

"When this house is quiet like this, a lot of times you can hear voices," shares Spradlin. "The cat will look around, stare at unseen things, as well." In addition, the spirits seem to enjoy messing with the inhabitants of their barn. Spradlin has several horses on their rural hobby farm and says that they "get flipped out" periodically over things that Spradlin cannot see.

It is not uncommon for Spradlin and others who visit the house to hear voices coming from out of nowhere. "It's like people are carrying on a conversation," she says, adding that she hears such voices "all the time."

"I love it," she admits. "I think it's fascinating. I'm not afraid of it. Why would I be? The house sings with all sorts of voices," she says. "If somebody wants to come visit, that's fine."

Chapter 34

McGuffy Hall at Miami U

When you gotta go; you gotta go. When you gotta go AND you're in class and you've got to plug some quarters into a parking meter AND only have a few minutes to do both and get back to the classroom in time? It makes for one heck of a mad race.

The year was 1998. Helen, an eighth grade history teacher from the Dayton area, recalls having one of those frantic moments while working toward her graduate degree at Miami University. The class was recessed for a few minutes and Helen had a dilemma on her hands.

"I remembered that there was this bathroom on the third floor of McGuffy Hall that was pretty secluded," she says. "I have a shy bladder," she adds with a giggle. She knew that nobody ever goes to that bathroom because it's the floor that the professors are all on. After racing to and from the parking meter, a wired Helen recalls witnessing the light at the end of the tunnel: the bathroom.

"I'm walking down the hall, and I watched a woman walk into that bathroom," notes Helen. "She had red hair; it was relatively long, and had on a long, cream-colored shirt." Helen was not pleased.

"Damnit!" she recalls thinking to herself. She knew there were only two stalls in that bathroom and realized if there was somebody else in addition to that woman she'd seen in there, she'd end up being late for her class. Toss in her bladder's shyness, and things were just not working out like she'd hoped.

Hoping that the redhead and herself were the only two ladies that had to use the facilities, Helen, who was about fifteen or twenty feet behind her, followed her inside.

"I got in the bathroom, and I am all alone," Helen says. There was no other way out of the facility other than the way she came in, yet the mysterious redhead was not in front of the sinks, nor in either stall. She was nowhere at all.

"I remember thinking, 'Okay…where did she go?' and feeling shocked at the whole incident. Now, I really had to pee," says Helen with a laugh.

Her grandmother was a comfort to her as a child, upon learning she was terrified of ghosts. "I just remember being terrified one day. I remember seeing something as a little girl in the hallway. I remember a guy in a striped shirt walking down the hallway and I was paralyzed, scared." That's when her grandmother told her there was nothing to fear.

"Helen," said her grandma, "you need to be more afraid of the live people, not the dead ones."

Her grandmother's wisdom helped the college student retain her composure following the sightings. "I did not see the redhead's face," says Helen. "I saw her hair, I saw her clothes, and I saw her walk into the bathroom (right before I did)."

"I went back to class," says Helen, "and I was shaken." It was very difficult for her to grasp what she'd just seen. She can still see this disappearing woman in the long, flowing skirt that came to about mid-calf. "I wonder if she had worked there at one time," says Helen. "She almost reminded me of a hippie. Maybe she was a student there at some point and maybe she's just still hanging around the teachers' college. That building is where the teacher majors go."

"Miami is notoriously haunted," says Helen, "But most of it's over on the western college campus." McGuffy is at the opposite end of the college, and Helen had never heard of any ghost sightings in McGuffy before or since.

But she knows what she saw and where she saw it. "I'm an eighth grade teacher with a masters degree, for crying out loud; I'm not supposed to be saying that we have sensitives (in our family). My cousin is sensitive, too (and helps family members locate lost items)."

The entire family bond for Helen is tight and her grandmother was a vital force in Helen's life, even after her death. One of Helen's first years teaching there was a problem concerning a certificate. Prior to her employers coming in to talk with her about this issue, she was overcome with her grandmother's scent (Wind Song perfume) in the classroom, which was empty, except for Helen. "My gosh, I smell my grandma! Where the heck is this coming from?" About fifteen minutes later, they came in and tried to fire her from her job. It was as if her grandmother came to support her.

"If we're having a bad day, ever since my grandpa died, we'd find dimes in the oddest of places. Once again, I was at Miami U and I was at the Shriver Center and they had a salad bar and I made a salad for myself and I sat down to eat it and I pick up my broccoli piece and there was a dime laying there in my salad.

"I live with the most giant skeptic on earth (her husband, Biff)," says Helen. "Orbs, I realize, take them with a grain of salt." But when

Odd face/forms appearing in the mist surrounding the little girls.
The children's grandmother lives next to an old Indian Burial Ground.
Submitted Photo (anonymous)

her youngest daughter was one and her other daughter was five, they had gone over to their grandmother's. The girls were running through the sprinklers and having a grand time in grandma's backyard (she lives on the golf course) while Helen took photos.

"I was thumbing through them as I took them," says Helen, "and I found one that just looked weird and I blew it up. There's an orb-shaped face between my child's legs," says Helen. "It has distinct features." She showed it to her giant skeptic and he said, 'Why is there a face on my child's legs?'"

To top it off, what looks to be a figure of water spray is hovering next to her other child. Helen admits it could be her brain trying to make something out of them but finds them fascinating, nonetheless.

The same giant skeptic, when he would drop off Helen at her parents' home before they were married, would periodically tell her that "I just have this awful feeling like I'm being watched. It creeps me out at night." He also thought he'd heard the sound of beating drums some nights. "I swear, I heard drums," he'd said.

They discovered, via an archaeologist, that there is an Indian burial ground smack dab at the end of her mother's street. Helen had asked the archaeologist how he knew it was a burial ground and not an observation mound? "It's from the sediment, the way the soil is packed together," the fellow had told her. "That's how we know it's a burial ground."

Helen has experienced multiple moments of awe, courtesy of her intuitiveness throughout her life and she is grateful for each and every one. Some helped her navigate the pain of her beloved cat passing, others just gave her a reminding nudge that our beings don't cease to exist once we leave this earthly plain.

Helen was with her grandmother when she died, as were other family members, and Helen recalls it as a "very beautiful, peaceful time. I felt like the live people weren't the only people in the room and I felt so much love." Even when her grandmother's breathing became extremely labored "it did not trouble me in the slightest," says Helen.

"There was so much love in the room and I knew we were not alone. I felt like her parents are here, all the people she loved are waiting for her, and it was very beautiful. Watching her pass away didn't make me fear death so much." Helen recalls feeling much the same way when her children were born. The processes of life from birth to death are incredible.

"If that is sensitivity, I guess I have it," says Helen. "I'm not nuts! I've just had some strange things happen to me in my life."

Chapter 35

Cynthia Lee
(Sees What Most Can't See)

Witnessing the other realm as most people cannot, is something that's been with Cynthia Lee, from Orgeonia, Ohio, her whole life. "These people (ghosts) are special to me," she shares. "Golly, that sounds rather weird doesn't it? I don't know how to put it; it's a bit of pride mixed with almost a mother hen feeling. Though I have had many separate occasions that I've seen ghosts, I want to go back again, but at the same time, don't. Usually the ghosts I've been scared of have been the ones I've seen more than once, so I'm a bit afraid I'd be very afraid the next time, or I won't see anything at all. But at the same time, that special feeling makes me want to go back, to let them know at least that they're not forgotten."

Lee has been witnessing paranormal occurrences for the bulk of her time on this earth (you can read about her accounts in Wright Patterson Air Force Museum in this book). "The first house my family built in Wilmington was built on haunted land," shares Lee. Haunted enough to pull forth distinct sightings of apparitions.

"There was a man that would pace up and down our hallway and sometimes I would wake up to him in my bedroom standing by the bed," notes Lee. "We didn't move from there until my sophomore year of high school and he scared me stiff!

"The second house we built in Wilmington had two places that were haunted. There's a tree across the street from the entrance of the building complex where I would see a gray horse and sometimes a man standing with it." In addition to seeing apparitions on a fairly regular basis, Lee has "heard" from the other side, as well.

"Down the road there was a patch of woods," she recalls. "I never saw anything, but there was a dead spot in the back corner that was cold and had a very bad feeling," she recalls. "When I got close to it the first time, I heard a woman's voice call out, 'Get out of here!'

Now, there were cornfields on all sides and the lots along the woods hadn't gotten sold, so no one was there to really yell at me, but I avoided that corner from then on. There was a very strong feeling of grouchiness along the fence of the woods. I got the impression of an old farmer or hunter, ball cap and red plaid shirt, though I never really saw him, and he was just grouchy. I felt sorry for him."

Whether home or away, Lee's radar is attune. "In Washington D.C., in the Octagon House, I was waiting for my mom to finish in the bathroom (which was downstairs) and I watched a shadow on the wall of a lady with big wide-brimmed hat with a feather come down the stairs, but, there was no (human) lady. This one I think is odd, because, while the Octagon House is said to be haunted, what I saw isn't one of the reported apparitions."

Closer to home, Lee says she's seen "shadows" flitting around the Murphy Theater in Wilmington, and says that those were "nice."

In Oregonia (right outside Waynesville), where we live now, there's a huge tree right against the road where supposedly there was a fatal car crash (I couldn't find anything to verify this though)," she notes. "Just last summer, I was taking the trash to the end of the driveway in a rainstorm just after dark. It was a little foggy from the pavement of the road being hot and it evaporating the rain as it fell. The fog in the middle of the road under this tree formed into a somewhat human shape that I could see well, despite the bad light." What or who was it? She doesn't know, but Lee is comfortable in the majority of her sightings and given her history, they will likely continue happening as the years continue forth.

Chapter 36

The Apparition of the House

"During the years when our son was in grade school and early junior high school, we shared some of our favorite autumn pastimes together," shares Dayton Ghost Hunter Society intuitive and member Connie Holder. "These soon became annual traditions. We visited pumpkin festivals and made the rounds of all the local haunted houses and haunted trails. He loved it so much that, when he was in high school, he worked at several haunted trails himself and took great delight in scaring the be-jeebers out of others. Of course, as he got older, he spent more time doing these activities with friends, but occasionally he would still let Mom hit some of the haunts with him. When he was about fourteen or fifteen, probably around 1991 or 1992, we had one of our most memorable nights ever at a haunted trail.

"Our favorite haunted trail, at that time for about three consecutive years, was the Haunted Trails of Sycamore Woods Park in Miamisburg, Ohio. This particular night in October was frosty cold and we were waiting in anticipation of some wickedly haunting fun on the trails. We weren't disappointed. We were first greeted by the persona of the Texas Chainsaw Massacre main character in the full 'persona' movie costume garb. We then proceeded through the dark and eerie wooded trails while being chased by a variety of ghosts, goblins, werewolves, vampires, and multiple chainsaw-wielding frightening characters. We ran and stumbled our way through the cobwebs and over the rutted trails breathlessly in giddy terror. Toward the end of the trail, we came upon a 'mock' car crash scene complete with wrecked cars, flashing lights, blaring horns, and many bloodied and screaming teens," notes Holder.

"Now we were headed toward the final scene of the haunted trail. It was a pretty impressive last 'jolt' (or so we thought) of the evening. As we were winding down a really steep hill," Holder recalls, "just before we hit the bottom pathway out, the 'bride of death' came flying out of the trees toward us and stopped just short of kicking us in the head. She swung wildly from a harness rigged beneath her gauzy bridal gown and ghostly white make-up.

"We had a lot of fun that night and were on our way out of the trails to call it a night and head for home. However, as usual, I had to use the restroom before our half-hour ride home. We had already used the restroom at Arby's, across from the park, before we went into the trails. We knew that they would already be closed due to the late hours and having inquired about their closing time earlier. That left us with only the park's meager bathroom facilities," she notes, adding, "This was not a prospect I was looking forward to."

According to Holder, "The layout of the park was such that the entrance was a long curving drive surrounded by woods on each side. Then it opens to a grassy area on the left with a large pavilion and then uphill into the haunted woodsy trail area. Farther on down on the left was a playground area. Even farther down on the left was a duck pond. Beyond the duck pond area was the bathroom and a small pavilion which were both in the most remote and isolated area of the park.

"It was a long, cold, dark walk to the bathroom and there was no lighting inside. My son didn't need to use the bathroom so I asked him to stay near the building and keep watch. I hurriedly used the restroom in the dark and re-joined him outside. When I came back out, I saw Andy staring off into the distance in an area behind and uphill from the restroom. My gaze followed his and we both stood transfixed by what we saw. There in the moonlight, up on a hill, we saw a large old house with at least two stories, old fashioned lamp fixtures, and some sort of porch.

"It was a very eerie sight," continues Holder. "I was particularly stunned because we had visited this park many times in the daytime and I had never seen this house before. It had such a large and eerie presence, I knew I wouldn't have missed it before. It was very solid and big but looked as if nobody was home. We both questioned each other as to what we were seeing and each confirmed that we were both seeing the same house. We both were a little 'unnerved' and decided to leave, but promised each other to come back in a few days to 'investigate' this place and check it out further. We talked about it with each other all the way home."

The duo kept the sight in their mindset and Holder recalls that about three day later, the mother and son returned to the park to get another look at the house and surrounding area.

The hill where Connie Holder and her son both witnessed the apparition of a house at the Haunted Trails of Sycamore Woods Park in Miamisburg. *Courtesy of Connie Holder*

"We were shocked and amazed to find absolutely no physical house there. There was indeed a grassy knoll in the exact spot we had seen the house," she exclaims. "We were of course trying to rationalize the fact that each of us saw the same house in detail a few nights before and yet here we were with nothing in sight during the day. We thought maybe, since a few days had lapsed, maybe they had torn down the ancient structure. However, the grass was all intact and fairly pristine. There were no remnants of a building of any type, no equipment, no rubble. Nothing, except the grassy knoll."

This was a huge sighting to be sure. Holder and her son were beyond intrigued; they had never heard of anything like that. "We returned a few other times over the years to the park, but never saw the house again," she says. "My son believes it was a real physical house that we saw. However, the only explanation I can fathom is that it was a full blown paranormal apparition of a house that was on the property years before, but had since been torn down.

"We have talked about the sudden appearance and disappearance of this paranormal house over the years and have never been able to come to a logical conclusion about it," admits Holder. "We had each mentioned it to a few others over the years, trying to see if anyone else had experienced it or could explain it. Most people were either as mystified by it as we were or tried to explain it away as part of the haunted trail, perhaps a hologram of sorts."

Holder goes on to explain that "that particular theory was not feasible, though, as the place where we saw the house was not even remotely close to the beginning, or ending of the actual haunted trail, due to the layout of the park. It also would have been missed entirely by probably ninety-eight percent of the patrons due to its location. So, what would be the point?

"Over the years, I had periodically gone back to the park hoping to see the house again, but always in the daytime. The last time we went, my husband Gary, a fellow DGHS Investigator, and son, Andy, and I all went together on a frigid day in February of 2008. I got out and snapped a few pictures hoping something paranormal would show up on film. Nothing showed up on the pictures so far, but I put them in a photo album along with some photos taken of the TAPS Ghost Hunters pictures we had taken at Wright-Patterson AFB, in January of 2008. I thought it would be fun to show them to our fellow investigators at the Dayton Ghost Hunter's Society Scare-n-Share.

"The next DGHS Scare-n-Share was held shortly after, at the purportedly haunted Amber Rose restaurant in Dayton. I passed the photo album around the table and two friends, Chris and Denise Corn (currently investigators in training with DGHS), and guests of fellow Investigator Penny Massie were visiting that night," says Holder. "They asked me why I had taken the pictures of Sycamore Woods and what significance they held. I told them about our eerie encounter of the full-house apparition in the park. Much to my surprise and delight, they told me that at one time there was indeed such a house. They said Chris had grown up and lived in the Miamisburg area most of his life and knew of the house and were familiar with all the pictures of the park. He said the house had been demolished years before."

According to Corn, his uncle had lived in the area and remembered the house and the pair had talked about that house, including when it was demolished.

"He said he knew that it had been torn down years ago, before the area had any restaurants. I asked them if it was torn down before Arby's was built and they said, yes, it had been torn down way before Arby's was built. Remember I said that Andy and I were in the Arby's the same night as we went to the haunted trail to use the bathroom. Their recollection of the house and time frame were enough confirmation for me at least that we had encountered our first ever paranormal house apparition," shares Holder. "Why it appeared to us, I guess we'll never know. I am planning on returning at some point after dark in hopes of capturing something on film this time. I was just so excited," relays Holder. "Over the years, my son and I have talked to people and relayed the experience and I got one of three responses: either, 'Wow, that's really cool...' or 'I think you've lost your mind...' or those who were just plain perplexed. Holder found it incredibly coincidental that she happened upon people who do recall the house that once stood there years before. It was an amazing coincidental validation. "My son and I are the only people I've ever known that have had a house apparition! It is unusual."

The unusual is fairly usual for Holder who is highly intuitive; so much so, she reads for others. "I do professional mediumship and intuitive readings, so I'm used to connecting with those on the other side. I can either hear them, feel them, or see them. If they're really strong, sometimes I'll get all three. I'm certified in clairvoyance (clear seeing), clairaudience (clear hearing), clairentience (clear feeling), and healing touch energy work." As is evident with Holder and her son's full-house apparition, however, "there is no guarantee what I'm gonna get and when I'm gonna get it." Who knows what the future holds?

Connie Holder can be contacted via her email address: Ibelieveinangels@woh.rr.com, and also through the Web site for The Healing Zone and Bookstore: http://www.thehealing-zoneandbookstore.com/.

Chapter 37

Potato Cakes and Poltergeists: Haunting of Arby's in Miamisburg

Some people are quite certain that something odd hangs around in the basement of the Arby's in Miamisburg. According to one daytime employee at the site, at least one of those people who has the night shift at the place is quite sure there is something down in the bowels of the restaurant and even in the kitchen, and has taken some interesting photos with her camera phone.

The hubbub over the potential paranormal inhabitants has not ceased and over the years; it has made several employees uneasy. They feel as if they are being watched. There have been reports of a man-ghost who is completely folliclely challenged. The peals of kiddies laughing and antics such as hair-pulling and things going missing have been reported. Also, moving shadows have been seen darting to and fro.

Just who or what might be inhabiting the basement of this popular fast food joint is unknown; it does seem an unlikely spot for a spirit to take root. Perhaps he or she was fond of the potato cakes while alive and couldn't bear to be separated from them forever? (If so, I can relate…)

Arby's Restaurant
in Miamisburg.

Chapter 38

Centerville Cemetery

The Howling of the Wolves...The Wolf Mausoleum

"Did you hear that? Did I hear that? That's wild!" Such are some of the remarks that surround the legend of the Wolf Mausoleum in Centerville Cemetery. Seems that the piercing and unnerving howling from the wild canines has been detected emanating from the small, unassuming cemetery in Centerville, Ohio.

It has been said that the Wolf Mausoleum is guarded by a duo of the creatures with the same name. The wolves were supposedly buried with their owner. The difference being, the poor canine-cousins were supposedly interred while still quite alive; directly in front of their master's mausoleum.

More than a few unassuming folks have reported hearing the piercing howls and have hightailed it on outta there at night.

Is this truth or fiction? Why not stop out some time and take a listen for yourself?

The Wolf Mausoleum at Centerville Cemetery.

Chapter 39

The Keifer Street Tracks

The Red-Headed Construction Woman

I had heard that people had seen an apparition along the railroad tracks and Keifer Street in Dayton. Seems they catch a glimpse of a red-haired, construction-hat-wearing lady loping around the tracks. Odd, huh?

Since we were already in the area, we decided to stop by the site, take a photo, and check things out. My husband waited in the car while I walked the short jaunt from the end of the road to the tracks, which were surrounded by woods on one side and businesses on the other. The side that I was on (the woods/neighborhood side)

The Keifer Street Tracks in Dayton.

showed obvious signs that the place was frequented by the home-less and/or drug abusers, including a bag of paraphernalia with what looked to be syringes inside. Despite this grim finding, it was a pretty, partly cloudy, spring afternoon and there was periodic movement/noise from the businesses across the tracks from where I stood. Oddly enough, given the time of day, activity and close proximity of my husband, I felt extremely uncomfortable standing on the tracks. When I held the camera up, it was at its most intense. It was almost as if I felt vulnerable to someone or something that might be lurking in those woods; something that could leap out at me. I told myself I was imagining these uncomfortable feelings (which, frankly, were out of the ordinary for me).

I must have sensed something because it was while snapping photos that I heard movement in the brush to my right. Whatever it was, sounded large; but sounds can be deceiving. My camera clunked to my chest (thank heavens it was connected around my neck) and I scanned the woods for any sign of movement—anything visible. I saw nothing and heard no more. I glanced back at my hus-band who seemed oblivious (nothing unusual there). I raised the camera up again only to hear movement coming from the woods on my left. Same sound; intense, loud rustling.

That was enough for me. I was back in the car without delay. No, I did not capture a full-body apparition of the red-haired woman in a hard hat that day. Heck, I didn't even nab a measly orb. Yet I included the Keifer Street tracks site in this book because of the sensations and feelings they elicited from me. Something felt different in that daylight; something I'd never quite felt before. I don't know what it was, but I do know I wouldn't relish the thought of returning there at night. (Or would I?)

Chapter 40

Woodland Cemetery

Talk a stroll past the gates and you will see that Woodland Cemetery is aptly named. This cemetery/arboretum located at 118 Woodland Avenue in Dayton is packed with soaring, 100-plus-year-old trees bursting toward the sky throughout the vast, rolling acreage. The cemetery, which was founded in 1841, is one of the five oldest garden-type cemeteries in America. Much as Spring Grove Cemetery in Cincinnati, Woodland holds numerous incredible monuments and outstanding botanical specimens alike, this does as well, plus the grave sites of numerous local and national dignitaries.

It is an arboretum as well as a final resting place and holds well over 3,000 trees and hundreds of species of woody plants. The hills in this cemetery are plentiful; many of them incredibly steep. So steep, you wonder how they finagled placing caskets within them. Several of the

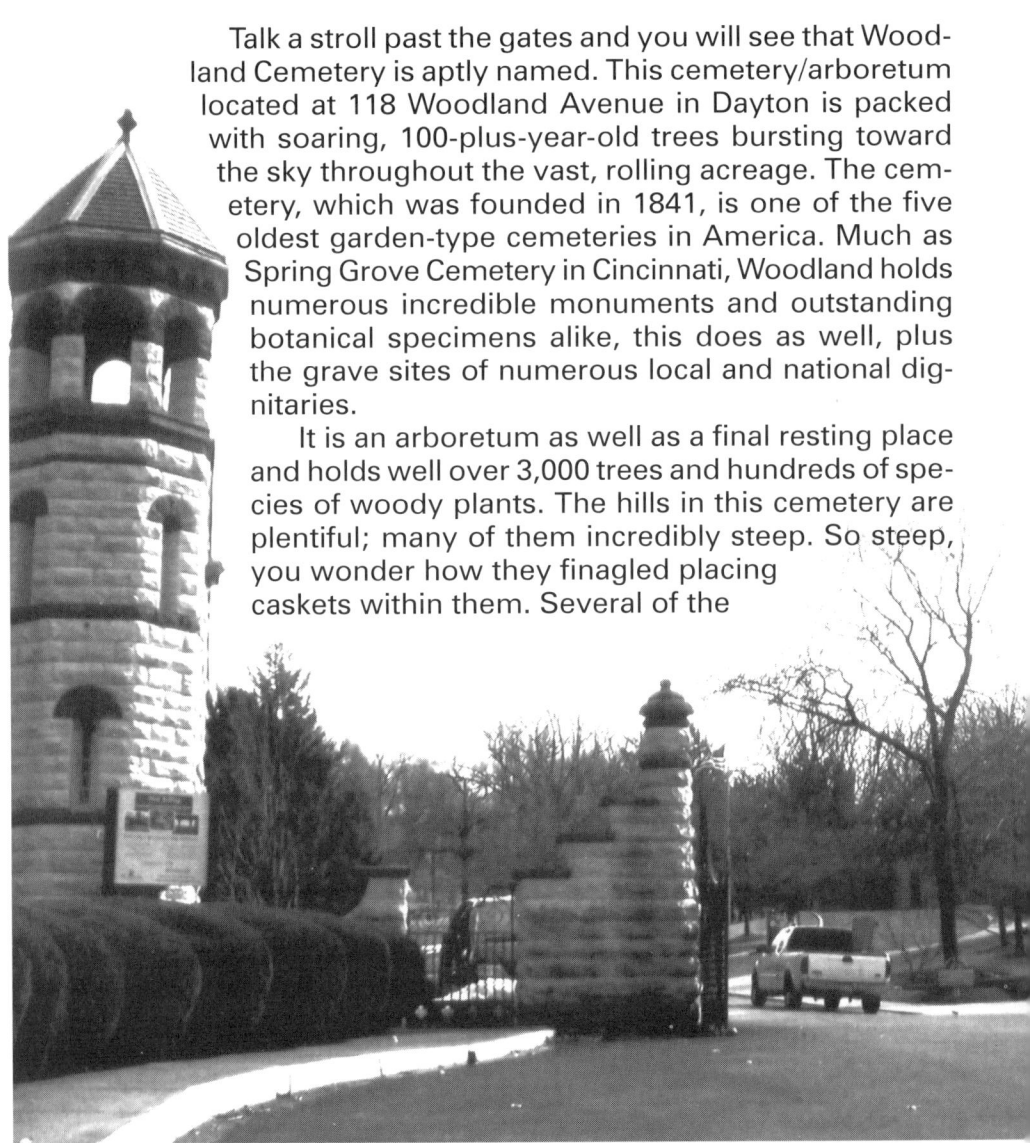

buildings, including the Romanesque gateway, the office, and the sublime chapel (erected in 1889), are on the National Register of Historic Places. Several areas of the cemetery are purported to be haunted as well. People come to visit their dead, get their exercise by running through the grounds, and many more come to tour the site where such notables as Wilbur and Orville Wright, Paul Laurence Dunbar, and Erma Bombeck are buried.

Bombeck is not believed to be haunting the cemetery, but since she is (and in my opinion, always will be) the reigning queen of family-based humor (a widely-read and renowned columnist and multiple-book author) and a true treasure of Dayton, Ohio, I would be remiss not to include her here. She wrote numerous best-selling

Woodland Cemetery in Dayton.

books and won the American Cancer Society's Medal of Honor in 1990 for advice to help children survive cancer. The humorist's grave is located close to the entrance gates of the cemetery and believe me, you can't miss it; it is marked by a 29,000-pound Arizona boulder (a rock-solid testament from her husband of the many years they spent living in Arizona).

Rest assured, however, that there certainly are numerous reports of hauntings at Woodland Cemetery. One of the more prominently mentioned ones involves that of a child. It is said that there is a young girl with blond hair, clad in blue jeans and white tennis shoes who is periodically spotted sitting on a cemetery marker. Students at the University of Dayton (which is located next to the cemetery) have seen the girl while strolling through the cemetery or sometimes have seen her while they are on campus, right over the fence. They say she talks to cemetery-goers who seem to initially believe this girl is of the flesh and blood variety; they don't realize she is a specter until after their encounter. Some believe she is forsaken because she is not buried alongside her father; but instead quite a ways away. The stone she's been seen resting upon has been noted to have an odd blue glow in the dark.

A Boy's Best Friend

The tale of Johnny Morehouse is bittersweet. It dictates the love and devotion of a canine to his young master, which continued well past his master's demise. Morehouse's story is from the 1860s. The boy lived with his folks in Dayton, in the rear of his parent's shoe repair store. When he was five-years-old, Morehouse was doing as many a child would do of that era, and even today—romping around the frozen banks of the Miami and Erie Canal. Tragically, Morehouse somehow ended up in the canal. His canine companion leapt into the canal after him and pulled him out. Unfortunately, the child was already dead from drowning and hypothermia.

Morehouse was buried in Woodland Cemetery but he was not left alone for long. It has been said that in the days following the lad's funeral, the dog showed up at the cemetery and sat upon his master's grave and wouldn't budge. Period. The dog would not move to get food or water; he just sat upon the burial plat of his buddy. People visiting the cemetery noticed this and some desperately tried to bring the devoted pooch some sustenance.

The grave sites of the infamous Wright Brothers: Orville and Wilbur.

Erma Bombeck's grave site at Woodland is one of the most popular attractions there.

Johnny Morehouse and his beloved canine companion are said to haunt the Woodland grounds. People leave gifts and change for the boy and his devoted dog.

The beauty and serenity that makes up the divinely haunted Woodland Cemetery in Dayton.

It wasn't long, however, when Morehouse's faithful dog succumbed to the lack of nourishment and/or the elements (or a broken heart?) and expired on top of his best friend's grave. It was said that folks were so moved by the dog's devotion that, in 1861, a monument was erected to depict the dog and the boy together. It shows Johnny lying in rest with his head upon his dog's paunch; the safety of his best friend's large paw protectively draped atop him.

The grave is a touching one to be sure and visitors to Woodland often stop by Johnny Morehouse's grave to bestow a toy or some other trinket for the dog/boy duo. Stuffed animals, tiny trucks and cars, little footballs, and flowers are strewn about. Johnny's dog has a faded green bandanna around his neck and a red hat is nestled atop Johnny's peacefully sleeping head.

The grave and the area surrounding it are colorfully filled with expressions of sympathy. Some people elect to leave coins and there is a woman who will periodically collect the money and purchase items for the grave. Johnny Morehouse and his dog are believed to still be hanging around Woodland today. The sound of a dog barking and even the site of a child and his dog cavorting through the cemetery grounds have been reported. Sounds like they truly are together forever.

The cemetery is a local landmark in multiple ways and tours are

available. There seems to always be something new unearthed at Woodland. It is a hauntingly wonderful Dayton treasure.

Web site: www.woodlandcemetery.org.

Bibliography

http://www.376hbgva.com/memoirs/rice.html
http://www.associatedcontent.com/article/747015/the_haunted_restaurants_of_ohio.html
http://www.britannica.com/
www.ci.dayton.oh.us
www.dayton.com
www.DaytonGhostHuntersSociety.com
http://www.daytonhistory.org
http://www.daytonhistorybooks.citymax.com
http://www.daytonohio.com/
http://www.daytonparanormal.org
en.wikipedia.org/wiki/Dayton,_Ohio
http://www.first-to-fly.com/Adventure/Expeditions/dayton.htm
http://www.flyernews.com
http://www.forgottenoh.com
http://www.ghostsofohio.org
http://www.haunted-investigators.com/
http://inventors.about.com/library/inventors/blignition.htm
http://journal-news.com
http://www.med.wright.edu/visitors/nearby.html
Ohioexploration.com
http://nl.newsbank.com/docs/DDNB/0FA3A4654BC3A309.html
www.sinclair.edu/
http://www.theamberrose.com
http://www.tourgreatmiami.com
http://www.usacitiesonline.com/ohcountydayton.htm#history
www.whisperingmoondesigns.com
wikipedia Dayton Ohio
http://www.woodlandcemetery.org
www.wpafb.af.mil/museum/
http://www.yourghoststories.com
http://www.zuko.com

Index